ECONOMIC ESSENTIALS

Delbert A. Snider
Miami University

GOODYEAR PUBLISHING COMPANY, INC.
Pacific Palisades, California

JUN 1 '72

Current printing (last digit):

10 9 8 7 6 5 4 3 2 1

ISBN: 0-87620-233-4

Y-2334-4

Library of Congress Catalog Card Number: 75-184517

Printed in the United States of America

HOW TO USE THIS BOOK

This book is intended to be a helpful aid to the beginning student of economics, who frequently becomes bogged down early in his first course.

Apart from the introductory chapter, designed to suggest methods of studying economics and to acquaint the student with the approach, terminology, and tools of the discipline, each chapter is devoted to a particular topic. Only the main theoretical topics of economics are included—applied and historical aspects are not considered. 1682442

Each chapter follows the same fixed format, in outline form, and is divided into four sections. The first section, "Principles," states in a succinct, summary fashion the *main conclusions* of economics with respect to the topic under discussion. This is designed to give the student a quick review of the topic, and if he understands the statements, he need not read further into the chapter.

If, however, the student is not sure of the conclusions stated in the first section, he should proceed to examine one or more of the other three. The second section, "Concepts," explains the meaning of technical terms used in stating the first principles. The third section gives a summary *explanation* of first principles. A final section, "Confusions to Avoid," seeks to identify the chief sources of misunderstanding which experience shows to be rather common among beginning students.

The most fruitful way of using this book may now be suggested. Let us say that the student has been assigned a chapter in his textbook, and that he has heard his instructor lecture on that topic. At some later time, possibly just before an examination (but preferably earlier), he reviews his notes and tests himself on his understanding of the subject. This would be the time to read the section on "Principles" in the appropriate chapter. Whether or not to refer then to the other sections of the chapter would be self-evident.

CONTENTS

HOW TO USE THIS BOOK   iii

PART I. BACKGROUND   1

1.   Introduction to the Study of Economics

How to Study Economics, 1   The Methodology of
Economics, 3   Economic Theory, 4   The Tools of
Economics, 5   Functions, 5   Graphics, 7   The Marginal
Concept, 10   The Relationship between Average and
Marginal Values, 13   Maxima and Minima, 14

PART II. NATIONAL INCOME ANALYSIS   16

2.   National Income: Its Meaning and Measurement

Principles, 16   General Definition, 16   Income
Measures, 16   Real Income and Money Income, 16
Aggregate Expenditure and the National Income
Equation, 17   Consumption Expenditure, 17   Investment
Expenditure, 17   Government Purchases, 17   The Foreign
Trade Balance, 18   *Concepts,* 18   The Measurement of
Income, 18   Components of Aggregate Expenditure, 19
Disposable Personal Income and the Consumption
Function, 20   *Discussion,* 21   Aggregate Output Equals
Aggregate Expenditure on Output, 21   The National
Income Equation, 22   The Consumption Function, 23
Investment and Government Expenditure, 23   *Confusions
to Avoid,* 23   The Difference between Real and Money
Income, 23   The Meaning of Investment, 24

3.   The Equilibrium Level of Income   25

Principles, 25   Definition of Income Equilibrium and
Disequilibrium, 25   Conditions of Income Equilibrium, 25
Concepts, 27   Planned versus Actual Expenditure, 27

Injections and Leakages in the Income-Expenditure
Flow, 27 *Discussion,* 28 The Role of Aggregate
Demand, 28 Demand, Supply, and Equilibrium, 28
Equilibrium Conditions, 28 *Confusions to Avoid,* 29
The Difference between Actual and Equilibrium
Income, 29 Equilibrium and Desired Income, 30

4. Changes in the National Income   **31**

Principles, 31 Disequilibrium and Income
Changes, 31 Changes in Autonomous and Induced
Expenditure, 31 The Income Multiplier, 32 Graph
of Income Change, 32 *Concepts,* 33 Leakages, Injec-
tions, and Equilibrium, 33 Autonomous and Induced
Expenditure, 33 The Marginal Propensity to Spend, 34
The Multiplier, 34 *Discussion,* 38 The Roles of
Autonomous and Induced Expenditure, 38 Self-Feeding
Income Changes: The Multiplier Effects, 38 *Confusions
to Avoid,* 39 The Propensity to Consume and the Pro-
Pensity to Spend, 39

5. Unemployment and Inflation   **41**

Principles, 41 Unemployment, 41 Inflation, 41
Deflationary and Inflationary Gaps, 41 *Concepts,* 42
Definition of Unemployment and Full Employment, 42
Meaning of Inflation, 42 Deflationary and Inflationary
Gaps, 42 *Discussion,* 44 Income and Employment, 44
Income and Inflation, 45 *Confusions to Avoid,* 45
Deflationary and Inflationary Gaps, 45

6. Fluctuations in Income, Employment, and Prices   **47**

Principles, 47 Cyclical Fluctuations, 47 The Main
Cause of Fluctuations, 47 The Acceleration Principle, 48
Turning Points, 48 *Concepts,* 48 Trend and Cycle, 48
Phases of the Cycle, 49 External and Internal Distrub-
ances, 49 The Acceleration Principle, 50 *Discussion,* 51
The Inherent Tendency Toward Income Fluctuations, 51
The Special Role of Investment, 51 Why Prosperity
(and Recession) Eventually End, 51 *Confusions to
Avoid,* 52 The Difference between the Multiplier and
the Accelerator, 52 Implications of the Business
"Cycle," 52

7. Countercyclical Fiscal Policy for Full Employment and Price Stability   **53**

Principles, 53   Meaning of Countercyclical Fiscal Policy, 53   Objectives of Countercyclical Fiscal Policy, 53   The Influence of Government Expenditure and Taxes on the National Income, 53   Fiscal Instruments, 54   Budgetary and Debt Implications of Fiscal Policy, 54   *Concepts,* 54   Countercyclical Fiscal Policy, 54   Full Employment and Price Stability, 55   Injections and Leakages, 55   Built-in Stabilizers, 55   The Government's National Income Budget, 56   *Discussion,* 56   The Role of Government Spending in the National Income, 56   The Role of Taxes in the National Income, 57   The Balanced-Budget Multiplier, 57   Fiscal Instruments, 58   Fiscal Policy and the National Debt, 59   *Confusions to Avoid,* 60   Fiscal Orthodoxy and Countercyclical Fiscal Policies, 60   Eliminating a Budget Deficit, 60

PART III. MONEY AND BANKING   61

8.   The Nature and Supply of Money

Principles, 61   Definition and Functions of Money, 61   Composition of Money Supply, 61   The Nature of Modern Money, 61   The Sources of Money Supply, 62   *Concepts,* 62   The Functions of Money, 62   The Nature of Bank Deposits, 63   *Discussion,* 64   Meaning and Nature of Money, 64   Coin and Currency Circulation, 64   Bank Deposit Creation, 65   *Confusions to Avoid,* 66   Demand Deposits and "Real" Money, 66   The Different Meanings of "Deposit," 66   The Dollar is Valuable Because of its Gold "Backing," 67

9.   Monetary Controls   68

Principles, 68   Absence of Effective Controls on Coins and Currency, 68   Limitations on Bank Deposit Creation, 68   Nature and Sources of Bank Reserves, 68   Federal Reserve Controls, 69   *Concepts,* 69   The Federal Reserve System, 69   Bank Reserves, 70   Member and Nonmember Banks, 70   Open-Market Operations, 71   The Discount Rate, 71   *Discussion,* 71

The Absence of Coin and Currency Controls, 71   The
Need for Reserves, 71   Reserves and Money Creation
by a Single Bank, 72   Multiple Bank Credit Expansion
in the System, 73   Sources of Reserves for the Sys-
tem, 74   Federal Reserve Controls, 74   *Confusions to
Avoid,* 75   Legal and Excess Reserves, 75   The Single
Bank versus the System of Banks, 75   Reserves and
Money Creation, 75

10.   Monetary Policy   **76**

Principles, 76   Money Supply and the National
Income, 76   Demand for and Supply of Money, 76
The Rate of Interest, 76   Countercyclical Monetary
Policy, 76   Monetary Policy versus Fiscal Policy, 77
Concepts, 77   The Supply of Money, 77   The Demand
for Money, 77   Transactions and Precautionary
Demand, 78   The Rate of Interest, 79   "Easy" and
"Tight" Money, 79   *Discussion,* 79   Money and the
National Income, 79   The Rate of Interest and Aggre-
gate Expenditure, 80   The Demand and Supply of
Money and the Rate of Interest, 81   Countercyclical
Monetary Policy, 82   *Confusions to Avoid,* 83   Money
and Income, 83   The Demand for Money, 83

11.   International Monetary Relations   **84**

Principles: Domestic versus International Money, 84
Foreign Exchange Rates, 84   The Balance of Pay-
ments and the Demand and Supply of Foreign Ex-
change, 84   Balance of Payments Equilibrium and
Disequilibrium, 85   The Rate of Exchange and the
Balance of Payments, 85   Correction of Balance of
Payments Disequilibrium, 85   *Concepts,* 85   Foreign
Exchange Rates, 85   The Balance of Payments, 86
The Demand and Supply of Foreign Exchange, 86
Balance of Payments Equilibrium and Disequilibrium, 87
Currency Devaluation or Depreciation, 88   *Discussion,* 88
The Balance of Payments and the Foreign Exchange
Market, 88   Balance of Payments Disequilibrium, 88   The
Rate of Exchange and the Balance of Payments, 89   Cor-
rection of Balance of Payments Disequilibrium, 90
Confusions to Avoid, 90   Foreign Exchange Rates, 90

The Balance of Payments, 91 "Balance" and "Equilibrium" in the Balance of Payments, 91

PART IV. PRICE THEORY   92

12.   Supply, Demand, and Price

Principles, 92 The Law of Supply and Demand, 92
Changes in Supply and Demand, 92 Price-Elasticity of
Supply and Demand and Price and Quantity Changes, 92
Concepts, 93 Supply and Demand and Quantities Demanded and Supplied, 93 Price-Elasticity of Supply
and Demand, 94 *Discussion,* 96 The Law of Supply
and Demand, 96 Changes in Equilibrium Price, 97
Elasticity and Price-Quantity Changes, 98 *Confusions
to Avoid,* 100 Demand (Supply) versus Quantity
Demanded (Supplied), 100 Elasticity and the Slope
of a Demand or Supply Curve, 100

13.   Theory of Consumer Demand   101

Principles, 101 Shape and Position of Demand
Curves, 101 Law of Diminishing Marginal Utility, 101
The Price-Elasticity of Demand, 101 Position of and
Changes in Demand, 102 *Concepts,* 102 The Law of
Diminishing Marginal Utility, 102 Substitution and
Income Effects, 103 Substitute and Complementary
Goods, 103 Income-Elasticity of Demand, 103
Discussion, 103 The Left-to-Right Decline of the
Demand Curve, 103 Determinants of Price-Elasticity
of Demand, 105 Determinants of Demand and Changes
in Demand, 105 *Confusions to Avoid,* 106 Changes in
Demand and in Quantity Demanded, 106 Marginal and
Total Utility, 106 Maximization of Utility, 107 The
Role of Substitutability, 107

14.   The Theory of Competitive Supply   108

Principles, 108 Market Supply, 108 Supply and
Profits, 108 Short-Run Competitive Supply, 108
Long-Run Competitive Supply, 109 *Concepts,* 109
Profits, 109 Marginal Costs, 109 Marginal Revenue, 110
The Short and Long Run, 110 Fixed, Variable, and
Average Costs, 110 *Discussion,* 111 Rule for Profit

Maximization, 111 Short-Run Supply, 111 Long-Run
Supply, 111 *Confusions to Avoid,* 113 "Economic"
Compared to "Business" Profits, 113 Maximum Profits
and Absolute Profits, 113 Short- and Long-Run
Equilibrium, 114

15. Productivity and Costs   **115**

Principles, 115 Productivity, Costs, and Supply, 115
The Production Function, 115 The Law of Variable
Proportions, 115 Returns to Scale, 115 Productivity
and Costs, 116 Short-Run Costs and Supply, 116
Long-Run Productivity and Costs, 116 Long-Run
Competitive Supply Curve, 117 Least-Cost Combina-
tion of Inputs, 117 *Concepts,* 118 The Production
Function, 118 Average and Marginal Products, 118
Fixed and Variable Inputs, 118 Internal and External
Economies and Diseconomies of Scale, 119 *Discus-
sion,* 119 The Law of Variable Proportions, 119
Returns to Scale, 120 Productivity and Costs, 120
Short-Run Costs, 121 Long-Run Costs, 122 Costs and
Supply, 122 Least-Cost Input Combination, 123
Confusions to Avoid, 124 Diminishing Returns and
Returns to Scale, 124 Minimum Average Costs and
Least Costs, 124 Long-Run Average Costs and Com-
petitive Supply, 124 Internal versus External Economies
and Diseconomies, 124

16. Output and Price Under Imperfect Competition   **126**

Principles, 126 Types of Market, 126 Costs and
Revenues, 126 Output and Price under Pure
Monopoly, 126 Output and Price under Monopolistic
Competition, 127 Output and Price under Oligopoly, 128
Concepts, 129 Demand, Average Revenue, and Marginal
Revenue, 129 Optimum Output and Price, 130 Entry
Conditions, 130 Product Differentiation, 130 Selling
Costs, 130 Price Wars, 130 "Kinked" Demand Curve
and Discontinuous Marginal Revenue Curve, 130 Price
Leadership and Other Pricing Conventions, 131 Admin-
istered Prices, 131 *Discussion,* 132 Declining Average
and Marginal Revenue, 132 Monopoly Output and
Price, 132 Output and Price under monopolistic

Competition, 134 Output and Price under Oligopoly, 135 *Confusions to Avoid,* 136 The Meaning
of Competition, 136 Maximum-Profit Price, 137

17. The Competitive Pricing of Factor Services   138

Principles, 138 Supply and Demand, 138 Demand for
a Factor Service, 138 Shape of the Demand Curve, 138
Elasticity of Demand, 139 Change in Demand, 140
Factor Supply, 140 *Concepts,* 140 Supply and De-
mand of Factor Services, 140 Marginal Revenue Product
and Value of the Marginal Product, 141 Elasticity of
Factor Service Demand and Supply, 141 Economic
Rent, 141 Classification of Factors, 142 *Discussion,* 142
Application of the Law of Supply and Demand, 142
Demand for a Factor Service, 142 Shape of the Demand
Curve for a Factor Service, 143 Elasticity of Demand
for a Factor Service, 143 Changes in Demand for Factor
Services, 144 Economic Rent and the Elasticity of Sup-
ply of Factor Services, 144 The Supply of Labor, 144
The Supply of Capital, 145 The Supply of Land, 146
Confusions to Avoid, 146 Factor Service Prices and
Factor Prices, 146 The Relationship between Output
and Input Approaches, 146 *Capitalization,* 147 The
Pricing of Factor Resources, 147

**18. Factor Service Pricing in Imperfectly
Competitive Markets   148**

Principles, 148 Forms of Imperfect Competition in
Factor Pricing, 148 Imperfectly Competitive Product
Markets, 148 Monopsony, 148 Factor Monopoly, 149
Bilateral Monopoly, 149 *Concepts,* 149 Imperfect
Product Markets, 149 Monopsony, 149 Monopolistic
Factor Markets, 149 Bilateral Monopoly, 149 *Discus-
sion,* 150 Demand for Factor Services under Imperfect
Competition, 150 Supply of Factor Services Under
Monopsony, 151 Bilateral Monopoly, 152 *Confusions
to Avoid,* 152 Interrelationship of Product and Factor
Markets, 152

19. The Market Distribution of Income   153

Principles, 153 Marginal Productivity and Functional

Distribution, 153   Determinants of Marginal
Productivity, 153   Effect of Imperfect Competition, 154
Personal Distribution, 154   *Concepts,* 154   Functional
and Personal Income Distribution, 154   Marginal
Product, 154   Technology, 155   The Distribution of
Factor Ownership, 155   *Discussion,* 155   Functional
Distribution in Pure Competition, 155   Determinants of
Marginal Productivity, 155   Effect of Imperfect Compe-
tition, 156   Personal Distribution, 156   *Confusions to
Avoid,* 156   Ethics versus Explanation, 156

PART V. PUBLIC FINANCE 158

20. Public Finance

Principles, 158   Roles of Government Expenditure and
Taxes, 158   Level of National Income, 158   Composi-
tion of National Income, 158   Income Distribution, 159
Principles of Government Expenditure, 159   Principles
of Taxation, 159   *Concepts,* 159   Types of Taxes, 159
Incidence and Shifting of Taxes, 160   Public Goods, 160
External Effects, 160   Benefit and Ability-to-Pay Princi-
ples of Taxation, 160   *Discussion,* 160   Level of
National Income, 160   Composition of Income, 160
Income Distribution, 160   Principles of Government
Expenditure, 162   Principles of Taxation, 163   *Confu-
sions to Avoid,* 163   The Various Functions of Taxes, 163
Public Goods, 164

PART VI. INTERNATIONAL ECONOMICS 165

21. International Economic Relations

Principles, 165   International Trade, 165   Law of
Comparative Advantage, 165   Bases of Comparative
Advantage, 165   Benefits of Trade, 166   International
Factor Movements, 166   Relationship Between Trade
and Factor Movements, 166   Effects of Trade and Fac-
tor Movements on Income Distribution, 166   Controls
Over Trade and Factor Movements, 166   *Concepts,* 167
Comparative Advantage and Disadvantage, 167   Rela-
tive Factor Endowments, 167   Factor Movements, 167
Tariffs and Quotas, 168   Terms of Trade, 168

Discussion, 168   Law of Comparative Advantage, 168
Factor Endowments and Comparative Advantage, 169
The Benefits of Trade, 170   Factor Movements Compared to Trade, 170   Effects of Trade and Factor
Movements on Income Distribution, 171   Trade and
Factor Controls, 171   *Confusions to Avoid,* 172
Absolute and Comparative Costs, 172   The Nation
versus the World,.172   The Individual versus the
Nation, 172

PART VII. ECONOMIC GROWTH   174

22. Economic Growth

Principles, 174   Meaning of Growth, 174   Long-Run
Perspective, 174   Elements of Growth, 174   Quantity
of Land or Capital, 175   Qualitative Improvements, 175
Efficiency, 175   Technology, 175   Population Growth
and Economic Growth, 175   *Concepts,* 176   Measurement of Growth, 176   Cyclical Fluctuations, 176
Capital, 176   Saving and Investment, 176   Technology, 176   Efficiency, 176   Malthusian Theory of
Population, 177   *Discussion,* 177   The Formation of
Capital, 177   Qualitative Improvements, 178   Economic
Efficiency, 178   Technological Improvements, 179
Population Growth, 179   *Confusions to Avoid,* 179
Cyclical Fluctuations versus Growth, 179   Benefits
and Costs of Growth, 180

CHAPTER **1** INTRODUCTION TO
THE STUDY OF ECONOMICS

*Economics does not have a reputation among most students for being a
"gut" subject. Nevertheless, for all but the few who find it totally incomprehensible, economics is an extremely valuable field to know about. The effort required to comprehend it may be great, but the rewards are commensurate. This
introduction will try to make the study of economics easier, more pleasurable,
and ultimately rewarding.*

HOW TO STUDY ECONOMICS

Many students begin their study of economics with the serious handicap
of having certain ideas on the subject already. It may seem strange that this is
considered a handicap rather than an advantage, but you must realize that a
great many of these preconceptions turn out to be erroneous, or, at best, half-truths. A learning process involving the eradication of previously acquired
notions is more difficult than starting fresh.

We make, then, a first suggestion: make a strong effort to "clear the
decks"; this does not mean you have to forget or eliminate everything you have
learned. But open your mind: when you encounter an idea which is strange or
conflicts with what you have believed to be true, make a special effort to comprehend it. *Comprehend*—that is, not accept blindly as gospel truth.

Much confusion and misunderstanding come from the failure to communicate. Economics, like all other disciplines, has its own language of specialized jargon. The language of the economist is strange: the words the economist
uses, with few exceptions, are part of everyday language; but frequently they

have quite different meanings in economics. Student beware and heed this lexicon:

Investment does not include stocks,
Nor saving money in socks.
Money in the bank is not what you think,
It is scratchings in blue and red ink.
Rent one pays since one must,
But it's really an unearned surplus.
Demand and supply are never equal,
Labor does not consist of people;
Competition in prices is great,
Of it General Motors does not partake.
Profits, firms would like to maximize,
But zero is enough for them to realize.
Marginal is a concept to be used with compunction,
For it's the first derivative of a function.

Save yourself the agony of, "But that's what I meant to say," by learning the technical meanings of specific terms and sticking with them.

Although the subject revolves around relatively few basic principles, economics is known for its many complicated conceptions and convolutions. The art of studying economics lies in identifying its *central ideas* and separating them from the peripheral and adjunctive aspects. These initial distinctions are performed in the following chapters in the sections labeled "Principles."

But this is the time to raise a warning signal. Economics cannot be absorbed by memorizing its principles. A certain amount of memorization—such as the precise meaning of various technical terms, of course—is unavoidable and even desirable. However, memorizing is not to be mistaken for understanding. Economics is highly analytical; it consists of logical statements about the interrelationships of key variables. The underlying logic must be perceived and understood, not merely memorized. This need to comprehend the logic of economics becomes increasingly apparent to the student as he digs more deeply into the subject.

Unfortunately, the light frequently comes on too late and too weakly, leaving unlit corners that obscure the picture as a whole. Economics cannot be understood as a collection of discrete pieces of knowledge. Our modern economy is not composed of compartmentalized segments: it is an organic whole whose various parts functionally interrelate. So, too, must the discipline which seeks to explain the operations of the economy be understood comprehensively.

The ideal way to learn economics (or any other discipline) would be to have one brilliant instantaneous flash illuminating all the corners. Unfortunately, there is no way of doing this; the limitations of the mind force us to approach economics bit by bit, bite by bite. In the jargon of the profession, this is closer to "partial equilibrium" analysis than to picture as a whole, "general equilibrium" analysis. More will be said on this subject later. At the moment, you can build up your knowledge of economics cumulatively, each newly earned part adding to previous ones. Not only is this necessary for understanding the subject, but it makes the process of learning much easier, and, for some, exciting. This is strongly reenforced by the symmetry of the principles of economics in their various applications. A good illustration is the theory of the household and the theory of the business firm. These two functional economic units behave in accordance with altogether different motives in different contexts. Yet the economic principles analyzing their behavior are essentially the same. If you understand the theory of the household thoroughly, learning the theory of the firm should be a snap, provided that what you learned earlier has not been put away in a separate compartment of your mind.

In approaching a topic it might be useful to read it over as quickly as possible, skimming over details. This provides a general overview into which the details can be fitted later. This also avoids the danger of failing to see the forest because of the trees.

THE METHODOLOGY OF ECONOMICS

Even if you follow the study suggestions—and additional ones your own ingenuity provides—you may still find economics a tough subject. "I studied hard and thought I understood everything, but . . ." sums up the most frequent plaintive expressions heard by economics instructors after examinations.

Apart from too little study time—concerning which nothing beyond clucking the tongue can be done—and improper techniques of study, two major causes of difficulties experienced by economics students are its methodology and its set of tools.

For many students, the approach to—or methodology of—economics is passing strange. This is especially the case for those whose background has been largely confined to the humanities and, paradoxically, the other social sciences. On the other hand, for those who have been exposed to the physical sciences and mathematics, economics is usually taken in stride. And this is the tip–off as to the "strange" methodology of the discipline.

Economics *is* a science in a more regorous sense than merely its formal criterion of objectivity would imply. In its subject matter, economics is most closely allied to political science, sociology, and history, practically without relation to the physical sciences. In its methodology, however, economics is closer to physics and chemistry than to the other social sciences (though this is becoming less true).

Economic Theory

By its nature, science is theoretical. All disciplines that seek to explain phenomena objectively share this characteristic and are to this extent sciences. A *theory* is an hypothesis about a cause-and-effect relationship. It is distinguished from a statement of fact such as, "It is raining." To say that it is raining because a cold front collided with a low-pressure center is to advance a theory.

No aspect of the world can be explained except in terms of theory. Yet the beginning student in economics typically exclaims that it is "just theory," with the implication that reality is something different. But what is economic "reality"? In a literal sense, it includes every situation and action of economic life, from the purchase of a piece of bubble gum to the decision of the federal government to spend an extra $10 billion. To bring meaning to the jumble of millions of individual acts, generalizations which capture central tendencies are required.

To cite an example, the theory of consumer behavior presumes that, among other things, *consumption expenditure* varies directly with *disposable personal income.* There may be numerous families whose behavior does not conform to this hypothesis. However, as long as aggregate consumption expenditure for all housholds taken together responds to changes in aggregate disposable personal income, individual deviations from the *general pattern* are not significant.

Needless to say, there are acceptable theories and unacceptable generalizations. An acceptable theory successfully predicts, within a reasonable margin of error, the consequences of given acts. Whether a theory is useful can only be determined by empirical testing. If the observation of actual events persistently contradicts a theory, it must be modified or rejected. This suggests that an acceptable theory must be capable of being refuted through testing. If a relationship is necessarily true by definition of the terms, it is not an operationally meaningful theorem.

Finally, a scientific theory is free of ethical or normative content. Theory is an effort to explain what is, not what ought to be. Since in concluding what ought to be value judgments cannot be avoided, these subjective conclusions have no claim to universal validity.

Theory necessarily abstracts from actual events and simplifies reality in order to arrive at useful generalizations. Such generalizations are especially difficult when, as in the case of economics, everything depends upon everything else. To fully explain any one part of the economic universe requires explaining it all. But this is not practical at a pedagogical level: it would require a *general equilibrium analysis* involving the solution of a multitude of simultaneous equations.

Fortunately, in most cases, a satisfactory approximation can be obtained through *partial equilibrium analysis.* The technique here is to identify the principal variables immediately relevant to the problem at hand, while putting other less important or remote influences aside. The common device employed to this end is the "other things being equal" (Latin, *ceteris paribus*) clause. The use of this phrase warns you that certain forces bearing on the problem are being ignored for the moment in order to isolate the influence of particular variables.

There are dangers as well as advantages in such procedures. For instance we say that the quantity of a good purchased depends upon its price—*other things being equal.* Undoubtedly price does exert a powerful influence on the quantity of a good demanded. But neither is there any doubt that other potent influences are present, such as income, prices of other goods, etc. Isolating the role of price becomes the purpose of the *ceteris paribus* clause. The danger, however, is that the other forces at work will be forgotten. In reality, other things rarely are equal.

The potential for reaching invalid conclusions on the basis of partial equilibrium analysis increases with the area enclosed in the *ceteris paribus* compound. For instance, in partial analysis it is assumed that demand and supply functions are independent of each other. This may be a perfectly valid assumption in one particular industry. It is not likely, however, to be valid for the economy as a whole or for important subdivisions.

The lesson to be learned from all this is the desirability of a combination of patience and wariness in the study of economics: patience with techniques demanded by the complexity of reality, and wariness of the dangers of oversimplification.

THE TOOLS OF ECONOMICS

We come now to the aspect of economics which many students find to be the most formidable of all—the tools of the trade. Like the physical scientist, the economist whenever possible quantifies relationships. An inevitable result is the application of mathematical techniques and, in empirical testing, statistical techniques as well.

Let the nonmathematically minded student not throw up his hands in despair! It is not necessary to be a mathematician to understand economics. Nevertheless, the study of economics will be much easier if some simple concepts and techniques are mastered at the outset. At the introductory level, the math required for understanding economics is minimal. Acquaintance with a few simple concepts is sufficient, and these are provided in what follows.

Functions

In seeking to explain an economic phenomenon, the first step is to identify the essential forces at work. The second step is to hypothesize what relationships these forces have to each other. Both these steps are embodied in a function.

A *function* is a mathematical statement of a relationship among interconnected variables, so that any given value of one of the variables implies a value, or set of values, for the other variables. For example, if Y is a function of X, then Y depends upon X in such a manner that for any value assigned to X a corresponding value is determined for Y. Conversely, any value assigned to Y implies some specific value of X.

If indicating a functional relationship without specifying its exact nature is desired, we write $Y = f(X)$, to be read "Y is a function of X." This tells us that for every value of X there is a corresponding value of Y, but imparts no further information. (Symbols other than f are also used to indicate a functional relationship—g, F, G, etc.)

The specific form of a function is given by an equation. As an example, consider the following:

$$Y = 1/2 X$$

This equation states that Y is equal to one-half whatever value is possessed by X (and that X is equal to twice whatever value Y has).

The application of the functional notation to economic relations can be illustrated in the theory of consumer behavior by the so-called *consumption function*. The theory expressed in the function is that, other things being equal, consumption expenditure depends upon disposable personal income. Letting C represent consumption expenditure and Y_d disposable personal income, the consumption function takes the following general form:

$$C = f(Y_d)$$

(Common practice is to write the function as $C = C(Y_d)$, where the C on the right side of the equation is used to denote the function.)

A specific consumption function may be found from empirical investigation. For instance, suppose that consumption in the United States is discovered to be equal to $10 billion plus three-quarters of disposable personal income. The equation expressing this would then be

$$C = \$10 \text{ billion} + 3/4 \, Y_d$$

In this case, the $10 billion is a constant, and the general form of the function would show the presence of a constant by the addition of another term—say A:

$$C = C(A; Y_d)$$

Graphs

It is frequently helpful, even illuminating, to see a functional relationship expressed in graphic terms. The usual economics textbook abounds in the use of graphic techniques.

As long as there are no more than three variables in a function, it can be expressed in graph form. Ordinarily, graphs are of two-variable functions, where the relationship between the variables is most easily seen.

The procedure for graphing a function will be illustrated by referring to the consumption function:

$$C = \$10 \text{ billion} + 3/4 \ Y_d$$

In the following table we first calculate the value of C for each of several values of Y_d:

Y_d	C
0	$ 10 billion
100	85
120	100
140	115
160	130
180	145

The next step is to set up a pair of *coordinate axes*—a horizontal X axis and, at right angle to it, a vertical Y axis. The point of intersection of the two axes is called the *origin,* which serves as the base reference point from which the variables are measured. Each axis is laid off in units of measurement.

The theory postulates that the *dependent* variable responds in a *passive* fashion as the result of a change in the *active independent* variable. Conventionally, in economics, the dependent variable is measured on the vertical axis and the independent variable on the horizontal axis, though there is no compelling reason for such an arrangement. Roughly, one may think of there being a causal relationship between the variables, with the independent variable acting as the initiator, or cause, of any change, and the dependent variable responding to it. In the consumption function, for instance, disposable personal income is regarded as the independent variable which determines the dependent variable—the volume of consumption expenditure.

Following the prescribed procedure, let us now measure disposable personal income along the horizontal axis, starting from zero at the origin and moving from left to right. Consumption expenditure is measured along the vertical axis, starting from zero at the origin and moving from bottom to top. The axes are laid off in units of measurement appropriate to the equation to be graphed. Refer now to Figure 1.1. Each axis is marked off in intervals of $50 billion. For ease of reference, lines have been drawn in at each interval, forming a grid. (If you use graph paper, this is already done.) Every point on a given grid line represents the same value of the variable being measured. For example, anywhere along the vertical line projected upward from the $50 billion mark signifies that level of disposable personal income; anywhere along the horizontal line at the $100 billion mark shows that constant amount for consumption expenditure.

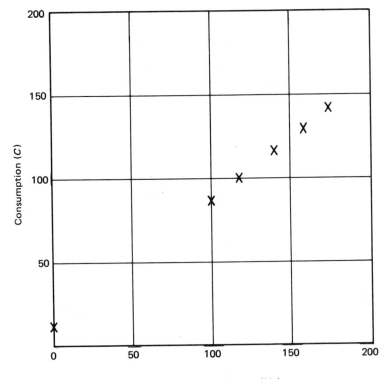

FIGURE 1.1 A Simple Point Graph

Any point in the plane bounded by the two axes represents a specific combination of disposable personal income and consumption expenditure. The X's inserted on the grid are the combinations of the two variables described in the table above. Reading from left to right, the first X is on the vertical axis itself at a point $10 billion above the horizontal axis. Hence, the X shows a combination of $10 billion consumption expenditure with a zero level of disposable personal income. The second X is on the $100 billion vertical line, $85 billion above the horizontal axis, and the remaining X's show the other combinations revealed by the consumption function.

The next step, shown in Figure 1.2, is to connect the X's with a continuous line (the grid lines have been removed to avoid cluttering the diagram). In connecting the X's into a continuous line, marked *CC*, we *interpolated* values for

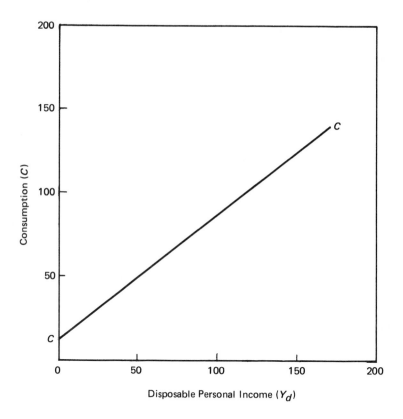

FIGURE 1.2 The Graph of a Linear Function

both variables within the intervals given by the X's. However, from the equation of the function, $C = \$10$ billion $+ 3/4 \, Y_d$, as many points as one wishes may be obtained by assigning different values to Y_d and calculating the corresponding values for C.

In the particular example we are using, it turns out that in fact only *two* points are needed to draw the consumption function "curve," for it is a *straight line.* In more technical language, the function is linear. All *linear functions* appear as straight lines when graphed on ordinary (arithmetic) scales. The graphical representations of other, nonlinear functions, assume a variety of shapes, depending upon the specific form of the function. The important observation, however, is that every function can be expressed in graphical form.

The Marginal Concept

As in other sciences, economics is principally interested in investigating the causes and effects of *change.* Economics studies why the national income rises and falls, what causes prices to fluctuate, what happens to costs of production as output is increased, etc.

There are three ways of measuring changes. The first is in terms of *total magnitudes.* The total costs of a firm changes as its output changes, for example, and we may measure this relationship through the *total cost function.*

If we let C represent total costs and Q the number of units of output, the total cost function, in its general form, is

$$C = f(Q)$$

Suppose that the specific function is

$$C = 5Q^2$$

In graphical form, this function takes the shape of the curve OC in Figure 1.3.

A second measure of change is in terms of *average values.* Average costs are the total costs divided by the quantity of output—or, in other words, *costs per unit* of output. Letting AC represent average costs,

$$AC = \frac{C}{Q}$$

If

$$C = 5Q^2, \quad AC = \frac{5Q^2}{Q} = 5Q$$

The graph of this average cost function is shown in Figure 1.4.

Finally, the third measure of change, and the one which plays an especially important role in economic analysis, is the marginal value. The *marginal value* is a measure of the *rate of change* in the total value.

For those familiar with calculus, the marginal concept is easily seen to be identical with the notion of the first derivative of a total function. Thus,

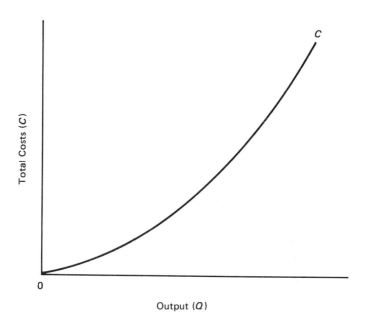

FIGURE 1.3 A Total Cost Function

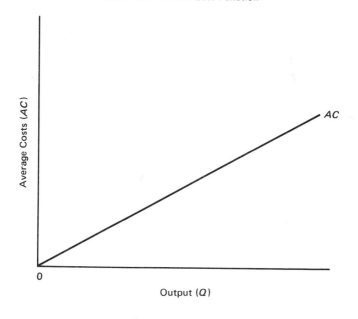

FIGURE 1.4 An Average Cost Function

marginal costs are the first derivative with respect to output of the total cost function. If the total cost function is $C = 5Q^2$, marginal costs (MC) equal $10Q$, and the marginal cost curve appears as shown in Figure 1.5, which also reproduces the average cost curve for comparison.

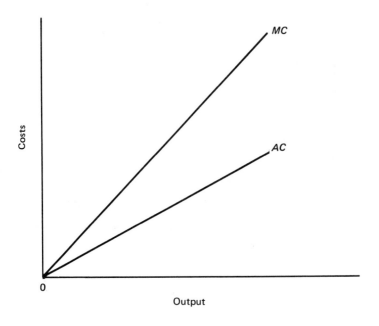

FIGURE 1.5 Average and Marginal Cost Functions

Since many students are not familiar with the calculus, the marginal concept is usually presented in textbooks in a less technical (and therefore less accurate) fashion. A looser definition of the marginal value is the change in total value *per small unit* of change in the independent variable. Thus, marginal costs under this definition are the change in total costs divided by a small change in output. Using the delta sign, Δ, to represent *change in,*

$$MC = \frac{\Delta C}{\Delta Q}$$

The accuracy of this measure of marginal costs increases as ΔQ approaches zero.

To indicate how marginal values may be determined without employing calculus techniques, let us apply the definition just given to the total cost function $C = 5Q^2$. The relationship between C and Q, and the associated relationship between ΔC and ΔQ, are as follows for selected output levels:

Q	ΔQ	C	ΔC	$\dfrac{\Delta C}{\Delta Q}$
10	–	500	–	–
	10		1500	150
20		2000		
	10		2500	250
30		4500		
	10		3500	350
40		8000		

The figures in the table for C are obtained by substituting the designated values for Q in the total cost function, and solving the equation. Thus, when Q is 20, $C = 2000$ for $C = 5Q^2$. Since the figures for ΔQ and ΔC represent *changes* from one total to the next, they have been inserted between the Q's and C's.

(Observe that the first derivative of the function, as indicated previously, is $10Q$, and that marginal costs as calculated by the above procedure fall in be-between the figures found by using the derivative. For example, at an output of 20, the marginal costs are 200, and at an output of 30, they are 300, calculated as ten times output. In the table, marginal costs are listed at 250 as output is increased from 20 to 30 units.)

Marginal values can also be derived through graphic techniques, as the *slope* of the straight line *tangent* to the total function. The slope of a straight line is the ratio of the vertical segment traversed to the horizontal distance covered in any movement along the line, such as a/b in the following:

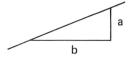

Thus, marginal costs at a particular output level can be found by drawing a line tangent to the total cost curve at a point directly above the specified output, and measuring the slope of the tangent line.

The Relationship Between Average and Marginal Values

Average and marginal values are mathematically related to each other in the following manner: when the average is rising, the marginal value must be greater than the average; when the average is falling, the marginal value must be smaller than the average; when the average is constant, the marginal value must be the same as the average.

Instead of proving those relationships mathematically, their rationale will be explained: Let us continue with the cost function as our example. For average costs to rise as output increases, the *additional,* or *marginal* costs, of producing an extra unit of output must be greater than the average up to that point, for these are what pull the average up. For example, with $C = 5Q^2$, average costs with $Q = 10$ are 50, and with $Q = 11$ average costs are 55. If marginal costs were the same as average costs when $Q = 10$—*i.e.,* 50— adding a unit of output would not change the average. The average rises from 50 to 55 as output increases from 10 to 11 because the marginal costs are greater than the average.

By the same reasoning, when average costs are falling, they are being pulled down by lower marginal costs; if average costs are constant, marginal costs are the same as the average—neither pushing up nor pulling down the average.

Maxima and Minima

One of the central principles of economics is the requirement for maximizing or minimizing some variable—the maximization of utility and profits, the minimization of costs, etc. Mathematics again provides the most precise techniques for determining maxima and minima, but since knowledge of calculus is necessary to use these techniques, we shall adopt another approach.

Suppose that the problem is to find the precise output of a firm at which the firm's total sales revenue is at a maximum. Let the total revenue function be represented by the curve *OR* in Figure 1.6. It is visually apparent that the

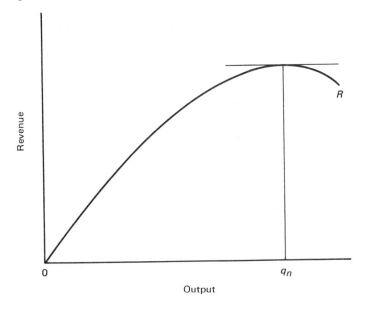

FIGURE 1.6 Maximum Revenue Output

revenue is at a maximum at output Oq_n, where the top of the revenue curve is reached. Now notice an important characteristic of the topmost part of the curve: the line tangent to the curve at that point is flat, with a slope of zero. But we just learned that the slope of the tangent to a total curve is a measure of the *marginal value* of the dependent variable. So, at the top of the curve, marginal revenue is zero—the general condition of maximum total revenue.

The logic of maximizing a variable by arriving at the point where the marginal value is zero is easily perceived. If the marginal value is greater than zero, increasing the independent variable by a small quantity adds the amount of the marginal value to the total value of the dependent variable. As long as marginal revenue is positive, total revenue increases with increases in output and sales, and therefore cannot be at a maximum. On the other hand, if marginal revenue is negative, decreasing output increases total revenue. Finally, when marginal revenue is zero, further additions to total revenue are not possible, so total revenue must have reached its maximum quantity.

A cautionary note: the criterion for a maximum total is identical with that for a minimum total, namely, a marginal value of zero. To distinguish between maximum and minimum values, an additional criterion must be introduced. Observe that in Figure 1.6 as the maximum revenue point is approached from the left, the total revenue curve is upsloping, while to the right of the maximum point the curve slopes downward. Precisely the opposite sequence holds for a minimum point, as can be seen by drawing a U-shaped curve. This, then, gives us the additional criterion needed: a marginal value of zero indicates a maximum total value if the marginal value is *positive* before reaching zero and is *negative* thereafter; a marginal value of zero indicates a minimum total value if the marginal value is negative before reaching zero, and is positive thereafter.

CHAPTER **2** NATIONAL INCOME:
ITS MEANING AND MEASUREMENT

A PRINCIPLES

1 General Definition

A country's national income (Y) is its *aggregate production,* or *output*, of goods and services during a given period (usually one year).

2 Income Measures

a. Measured on a gross basis and at market prices, the national income is called the *gross national product (GNP)*.

b. Measured on a net basis and at market prices, the national income is called the *net national product (NNP)*.

c. Measured on a net basis and at *factor costs,* the national income is called the *national income at factor costs* (Y_F).

(NOTE: The same analytical principles apply to all three measures of national income. Hence, the term *national income,* represented by the symbol Y will be used, unless specifically noted otherwise, in its generic sense.)

3 Real Income and Money Income

The *real* national income consists of the physical output of goods and services. The *money* national income consists of expenditures on the output of goods and services.

The real national income and the money national income are identical over any period during which the value of the dollar remains constant. But if the value of the dollar varies from one period to another, changes in money income will differ from changes in the real income. In this case, money income changes must be "deflated" in order to measure real income changes.

4 Aggregate Expenditure and the National Income Equation

The output of goods and services (national income) is equivalent to *aggregate expenditure* on newly produced goods and services. Aggregate expenditure is composed of:

consumption expenditure (C),
investment expenditure (I),
government purchases of goods and services (G), and
foreign trade balance—that is, exports (X) minus imports (M).

This yields the *national income equation:*

$$Y = C + I + G + (X\text{-}M)$$

5 Consumption Expenditure

The level of *consumption expenditure* (C) is determined by variables such as the amount and distribution of wealth, the rate of interest, and attitudes toward thrift. However, the most important variable is the level (and distribution) of *disposable personal income* (DPY). The relationship between consumption and disposable personal income is defined by the consumption function.

6 Investment Expenditure

Investment expenditure (I) is determined, in general, by expectations about future rates of return on investments compared with the investment costs. Such things as technological developments, rate of population growth, the cost of borrowed money (the interest rate), the present and expected future level of national income and consumption, etc., exert important influences on investment decisions.

7 Government Purchases

In general, *government expenditure* (G) on goods and services depends upon currently accepted social and political ideas about the proper role of government in the economy. Within this context, the accepted "need" for government pur-chases depends upon rate of population growth, urbanization, rate of income growth, etc. Expenditures are also subject to large-scale changes in response to international political and military developments.

8   The Foreign Trade Balance

Exports (X) and imports (M) are responsive to numerous forces, domestic and foreign. Given the role of foreign trade in the structure of the national econ-omy, the most important determinants of exports are the levels of income and prices in other countries; the most important determinants of imports are the levels of income and prices in the home country.

B   CONCEPTS

1   The Measurement of Income

a. In order to measure the aggregate output of the widely diverse goods and services produced in the national economy, a common unit of measure-ment is required. This is provided by the *dollar value* of the goods and services.

   The valuation of income at *market prices* means that goods and ser-vices are included in income at the prices actually paid for them in the market, including any excise, sales, or other so-called "indirect business taxes."

   The valuation of income at *factor costs* excludes the indirect busi-ness taxes from market prices. Income valued at factor costs is equal to the sum of wages, interest, rents, and profits earned in production—or, when stated on a net basis, the *national income at factor costs* (Y_F).

b. *Gross* income is larger than *net* income by the amount of *depreciation* of plant and equipment incurred in producing the goods and services comprising the national income. The gross national product (*GNP*) is calculated without deducting depreciation (*D*); the net national prod-uct (*NNP*) is arrived at by making such a reduction. Hence,

$$GNP = NNP + D$$

or

$$NNP = GNP - D$$

The national income at factor costs (Y_F), like the net national product, is on a net basis.

In summary, the *GNP* is the broadest measure of national income: it includes both depreciation and indirect business taxes. The *NNP* is next broadest, including indirect business taxes but excluding depreciation. The Y_F is the narrowest measure, since it includes neither indirect business taxes nor depreciation. The differences among the three income measures are shown as follows:

$$GNP - D = NNP$$

$$NNP - \text{indirect business taxes} = Y_F$$

c. To correct (or "deflate") money income changes to measure real income changes, calculate the change(s) in the value (purchasing power) of the dollar.

The value of the dollar during one period, T_1, is expressed in terms of its value during another period, T_2, by dividing the index of prices in period T_2 (P_2) by the index of prices in period T_1 (P_1).

For example, suppose that the index of prices is 100 in T_1 and 125 in T_2. Then the value of the dollar in T_1 is 125/100 times its value in T_2, or 1.25 as great. Conversely, the value of the dollar in T_2 is 100/125 times its value in T_1, or 8/10 (4/5) as great.

With the relationship between the value of the dollar found in two different periods, the money national income for these periods can be expressed in the dollars of *one* of the periods—which one does not matter, since the only requirement is that both periods' income be expressed in dollars of the same value.

For example, let the money national income be $400 billion in T_1 and $600 billion in T_2. If the value of the dollar in T_1 is 125/100 times its value in T_2 (and T_2's dollar is 8/10 the value of T_1's dollar), then T_1's income expressed in T_2 dollars is $500 billion (400 × 125/100). Comparing this with T_2 income of $600 billion shows an increase in *real* income of 100/500, or 20 percent. The same answer can be found by converting T_2's income into T_1 dollars (600 × 8/10 = 480) and comparing this figure with $400 billion, yielding 480/400, an increase of 80/400 = 20 percent.

2 Components of Aggregate Expenditure

a. *Consumption* expenditure means expenditure on goods and services for the final use of individuals. One exception: the purchase of a new house is classified as an investment rather than consumption expenditure.

b. *Investment* expenditure is outlay on goods produced during the year which are added to the stock of goods in existence. It includes expenditures on plant and equipment, inventories, and residential housing as major components. It does *not* include the purchase of stocks and bonds and other purely financial transactions in "paper" claims and evidences of debt or ownership.

c. *Government* expenditure is only that portion of total government (federal, state, and local) spending which is on goods and services. Excluded are so-called "transfer payments," social security benefits, pensions, subsidies, interest on the national debt, etc.

d. Exports are domestically produced goods and services that are sold abroad. Imports are foreign-produced goods and services the country purchases from abroad.

3 Disposable Personal Income and the Consumption Function

a. *Disposable personal income (DPY)* is that part of the net national income ending up in the hands of individuals, which individuals are free to dispose of as they see fit.

Beginning with the gross national product, several deductions (and one addition) are required to arrive at disposable personal income. The first deduction is depreciation, since *DPY* is on a net basis. Indirect business taxes must be deducted, for they become government revenue, not personal income. The same is true of corporate income taxes and payroll taxes (social security contributions). Finally, undistributed corporate profits—or business saving—need to be subtracted. The one addition is transfer payments, for these are not included in the national income, but are regarded as personal income.

After all these adjustments are made, there remains *personal income (PY)*. From personal income are deducted personal taxes to arrive at disposable personal income. A tabular summary of the required adjustments is:

$$
\begin{aligned}
GNP &- \text{depreciation} = NNP \\
&- \text{indirect business taxes} = Y_F \\
&- \text{corporate income taxes} \\
&- \text{payroll taxes} \\
&- \text{undistributed corporate profits} \\
&+ \text{transfer payments} = PY \\
&- \text{personal taxes} = DPY
\end{aligned}
$$

b. Individuals use disposable personal income in only two ways: consumption expenditure (C) and personal saving (PS). Hence,

$$DPY = C + PS$$

The *consumption function* states the relationship between the amount of disposable personal income and consumption. The general form of the function is

$$C = f(DPY)$$

which merely means that C is dependent upon DPY and varies with it in some particular way.

A hypothetical example of a specific consumption function is:

$$C = \$100 \text{ billion} + 9/10\, DPY$$

This states that consumption expenditure equals $100 billion plus 9/10 of whatever level of disposable personal income prevails. Since that portion of disposable personal income *not* spent on consumption is, by definition, personal saving, complementary to the consumption function is the *personal saving function:* $PS = \phi(DPY)$.

Thus, if $C = \$100 + 9/10\, DPY$

$$S = DPY - C$$

$$= DPY - (\$100 + 9/10\, DPY)$$

$$= -\$100 + 1/10\, DPY$$

The consumption and personal saving functions are shown graphically in Figure 2.1.

CC is the consumption function, SS the personal saving function. The 45° line is merely a "helping" line for reference. At the point where CC crosses the 45° line, *all* disposable personal income is consumed, thus personal saving is zero and the SS line crosses the base axis.

C   DISCUSSION

1   Aggregate Output Equals Aggregate Expenditure on Output

Output can be measured meaningfully only in terms of its dollar value in the market.

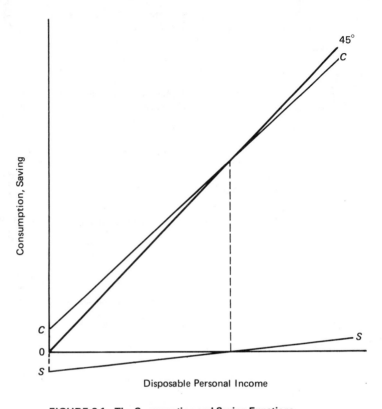

FIGURE 2.1   The Consumption and Saving Functions

But market value is the same thing as the price paid for a good or service, so aggregate output is measured by aggregate expenditure on the output. (NOTE: If a good is produced by a firm but not sold to its customers during the year, the value is equal to what the firm paid out in wages, interest, etc. to produce it.)

2   The National Income Equation

Since the *national income equation,*

$$Y = C + I + G + (X - M)$$

is a definitional statement of the national income, it necessarily holds true. (Accordingly, it would be appropriate to regard the equation as an identity and connect the two sides with a triple bar instead of the double-barred equals sign.)

The terms $(X-M)$ representing the foreign trade balance may need a word of explanation. Exports enter into the national income positively, for they are part of the domestic output, even though consumed abroad. Imports are a negative entry since that part of domestic expenditure which is not for domestically produced goods and services is not included in the national income.

3 The Consumption Function

The primary basis for accepting the *consumption function* is observed behavior. If data on consumption expenditure are plotted against disposable personal income, a remarkably close correlation is obtained for most periods. A curve of "best fit" showing the relationship between consumption and disposable personal income for past periods may be derived by statistical techniques (for example, least–squares regression analysis). The resulting consumption function line displays great short-run stability in the United States economy.

The rationale of the theory that consumption depends upon disposable personal income is simply that income sets a limit on the ability of individuals to spend without going into debt or liquidating assets.

4 Investment and Government Expenditure

In contrast to consumption, which is regarded as largely dependent upon income, *investment expenditure* is to a great extent independent of current income, or autonomous. This is so partly because expected future income—returns on investment—is more relevant than present income. Like investment, *government purchases* of goods and services are also largely autonomous—*i.e.*, independent of the current level of income.

D CONFUSIONS TO AVOID

1 The Difference between Real and Money Income

While the money value of (equal to the expenditure on) output is the only way of measuring real income, it must be kept in mind that real income *consists* of the goods and services themselves. Also, when comparisons are made between different periods, it is usually necessary to correct the money values of output for any changes in the price level in order to obtain a valid measure of changes in real income.

2 The Meaning of Investment

The term *investment* in national income analysis should be kept clearly separate from the popular meaning (referring to the purchase of any asset, including stocks, bonds, mortgages, and other paper claims, which yields or is expected to yield income, or is expected to increase in monetary value).

In its economic sense, investment refers to that portion of national output which is used to replace depreciated capital equipment and/or which is added to the stock of goods in existence. If only worn-out plant and equipment are replaced, net investment is zero (and gross investment equals the replacement). If there is an *addition* to the stock of goods, over and above replacing used-up capital goods, the addition constitutes positive net investment.

A   PRINCIPLES

1   Definition of Income Equilibrium and Disequilibrium

a. *Income equilibrium* exists when the interrelationship among the variables determining the national income is such that no forces operate to cause a change in the level of income.

b. *Income disequilibrium* prevails when the relevant variables are so related that the level of income tends to change.

2   Conditions of Income Equilibrium.

a. *Income equilibrium* is established when aggregate planned expenditure on goods and services is equal to current aggregate output of goods and services—in short, when aggregate demand (D_A) equals aggregate supply (S_A). This in turn occurs when *injections* into the income-expenditure stream—consisting of planned investment (I_p), government purchases (G), and the foreign trade balance $(X-M)$—equal *leakages* from the income-expenditure stream, consisting of planned saving (S_p) and taxes (T). Hence, the following is the *income–equilibrium equation*:

$$S_p + T = I_p + G + (X-M)$$

The equilibrium equation may be rewritten by subtracting taxes (T)

from both sides:

$$S_p = I_p + (G-T) + (X-M)$$

If the equilibrium equation does not hold, there is income *disequilibrium,* and the level of income can be expected to change. If leakages exceed injections (*i.e.,* the left side of the equilibrium equation exceeds the right side), the national income tends to *decline.* If injections exceed leakages, the national income tends to *increase.*

b. **Graphical representation of equilibrium**

In Figure 3.1, the aggregate output of goods and services is measured on the horizontal axis. The vertical axis measures planned aggregate expenditure (along the *EE* line), injections into the income stream (along the line labeled $I_p + G + X-M$), and planned saving and taxes (along the line marked $S_p + T$). The diagonal 45° line is provided as a reference base.

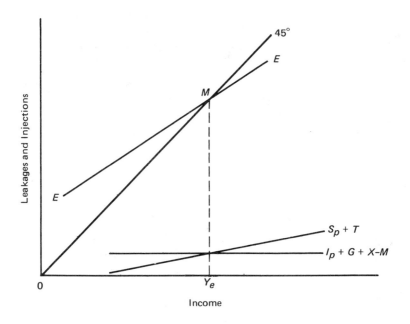

FIGURE 3.1   Income Equilibrium

The equilibrium condition where output (aggregate supply) is equal to planned expenditure on the output (aggregate demand) is satisfied only at point *M,* where *EE* crosses the 45° line. Correspondingly, OY_e

is the equilibrium level of national income, for only at income OY_e does aggregate demand (equal to Y_eM) equal aggregate supply (equal to OY_e).

The alternative designation of equilibrium is shown in the lower part of the figure at the point of intersection of the injections line ($I_p + G + X$-M) and the leakages line ($S_p + T$).

Observe that the intersection of the lines of injections and leakages occurs at the same income level where the aggregate planned expenditure line EE crosses the 45° line.

B   CONCEPTS

1   Planned versus Actual Expenditure

Recall: the national income is equal to aggregate expenditure on goods and services produced during the year (see Chapter 2). This is expressed in the national income equation, or identity:

$$Y = C + I + G + (X-M)$$

Each expenditure component of this equation represents *actual, realized* expenditure, whether planned or not.

The important difference that may arise between actual and planned expenditure can be illustrated in relation to investment in inventories.

Suppose that a manufacturer plans, for a forthcoming year, to keep his inventory of finished goods on hand at a beginning level of $100 thousand. Assume that the company expects to sell $500 thousand worth of goods during the year and produces this quantity, expecting thereby neither to add to nor to draw down its inventory. Suppose now that the company succeeds in selling only $400 thousand worth of its output of $500 thousand. As a consequence $100 thousand of its output is added to inventory. This represents an investment, but one that was unintended and unplanned. The firm's output contributed $500 thousand to the year's national income, equal to the actual expenditure on the goods ($400 thousand by the customers of the firm, plus $100 thousand by the firm itself), but there was only $400 thousand of *planned* expenditure contributing to *aggregate demand* for output.

2   Injections and Leakages in the Income–Expenditure Flow

The production of goods and services creates an equivalent amount of income receipts. Receivers of income spend some portion of it on consumer goods and services, creating a demand for output. But another portion of income is *not* spent on consumption, going instead into *taxes* and *planned saving*. Thus, that portion of income receipts paid in taxes and devoted to planned saving does not reappear as *demand for output*. For this reason, taxes and planned saving are called *leakages* in the income–expenditure stream.

On the other hand, consumption expenditure does not constitute the only demand for output. Planned investment expenditure, government purchases of goods and services, and any excess of exports over imports also produce aggregate demand for output. These form the counterpart, the "demand-creation" side, whereas tax and planned-saving leakages comprise the "demand-destruction" side; they are therefore labeled *injections* into the income-expenditure stream. If total injections happen to equal total leakages, the demand for output equals the output, and the national income is in equilibrium.

C   DISCUSSION

1   The Role of Aggregate Demand

Within the limits set by the productive capacity of an economy, output depends upon *demand*. Except for the public services directly rendered by government, the national output is produced by private business firms in search of profits. Profits are received from the production and sale of goods and services. If demand for goods and services increases, expressed in greater planned expenditure, the normal response of business firms is to increase output. (If output cannot be increased because of capacity limitations, increased expenditure causes prices to rise, raising the *money* national income without increasing the *real* national income.) By the same token, a decrease in aggregate demand normally leads to a cutback in production and income.

2   Demand, Supply, and Equilibrium

The actual output of goods and services during any given year is the country's national income for that year. It is also the *supply* of currently produced goods and services. If individuals and households, business firms, and government desire to purchase the actual current output of goods and services— no more nor less—aggregate demand and supply will match, so that there is no motive either to increase or decrease the level of current production and income equilibrium prevails.

3   Equilibrium Conditions

Aggregate demand will equal aggregate supply (creating income equilibrium) if injections into the income–expenditure stream—$I_p + G + (X-M)$—equal leakages from the stream, $S_p + T$. The proof is as follows:

$$\text{Aggregate supply } (S_A) = \text{actual production} = Y$$

$$\text{Aggregate demand } (D_A) = Y - T - S_p + I_p + G + X - M$$

(NOTE: $Y - T - S_p$ is equivalent to consumption expenditure, since consumption is equal to the national income minus taxes and planned saving.)

$$\text{If } S_A = D_A,$$

$$Y = Y - T - S_p + I_p + G + X - M$$

and therefore

$$Y - (Y - T - S_p + I_p + G + X - M) = 0$$

The Y's cancel, leaving

$$T + S_p - I_p - G - X + M = 0$$

Transferring all terms except T and S_p to the right side, we obtain

$$T + S_p = I_p + G + X - M$$

which is the equilibrium equation.

The above relations may be expressed as: actual output, equal to national income or aggregate supply, generates an equivalent amount of income receipts. A portion of income receipts is paid in taxes, another is devoted to planned saving. The remainder is spent on consumption, which is the first component of aggregate demand. For total aggregate demand to equal aggregate output, that part of income *not* spent on consumption—namely, taxes plus planned saving—must be matched by the other components of aggregate demand—planned investment, government purchases, plus the foreign trade balance.

D   CONFUSIONS TO AVOID

1   The Difference between Actual Income and Equilibrium Income

For any given period, the national income is, by definition, the aggregate *actual,* or realized, expenditure on the goods and services produced during that period. This relationship is summarized in the identity:

$$Y \equiv C + I + G + (X-M)$$

Corresponding to this is a second identity:

$$Y \equiv C + T + S$$

This identity must hold, since the aggregate income receipts generated by production are entirely accounted for by consumption expenditure, taxes, and saving.

Combining these two identities and eliminating the common term C yields a third identity:

$$S + T \equiv I + G + (X-M)$$

These three relationships must hold true definitionally. In contrast, the *equilibrium* equation, $S_p + T = I_p + G + (X-M)$, holds true only under very special conditions. The equilibrium equation is precisely the same as the third form of the expenditure identity, except for the subscript "p" attached to S and I. The significance of the subscript is its indication that saving and investment are *planned*, or intended, as contrasted to *actual*, or realized. If it should happen that actual $S + I$ are each the same as planned $S + I$, then the identity and the equilibrium equation would be the same, and the actual level of income would be the equilibrium level.

2 Equilibrium and Desired Income

Equilibrium in economics is an analytical concept without inherent ethical values. Do not, therefore, look upon equilibrium in income as being "good" or "bad"; rather, it is a state of rest from which there is no tendency for income changes to occur.

CHAPTER 4

CHANGES IN THE NATIONAL INCOME

A PRINCIPLES

1 Disequilibrium and Income Changes

National income changes as a consequence of being in disequilibrium—*i.e.*, because of an inequality between leakages in the income-expenditure stream $(S_p + T)$ and injections into it $(I_p + G + X\text{-}M)$.

If $S_p + T > I_p + G + X\text{-}M$, income tends to decrease.

If $I_p + G + X\text{-}M > S_p + T$, income tends to increase.

2 Changes in Autonomous and Induced Expenditure

a. Starting from a given equilibrium level of income, a movement in income is initiated by an *autonomous change* in expenditure.

b. Autonomous changes in expenditure generate additional, *induced* changes in expenditure and income.

c. The *total* change in income initiated by autonomous movements equals the sum of the change in autonomous expenditure plus changes in induced expenditure. Letting the delta sign, Δ, represent *change in; Y, income* or *expenditure;* E_A *autonomous expenditure;* and E_i *induced expenditure:*

$$\Delta Y = \Delta E_A + \frac{\Delta E_i}{\Delta Y} \cdot \Delta Y$$

3   The Income Multiplier

a. The national *income multiplier* is the number by which an autonomous change in expenditure is multiplied to arrive at the total change in income ultimately occurring as a result of this autonomous expenditure change.

b. The multiplier effect is caused by induced expenditure. The greater the induced expenditures are, the larger the multiplier. Since the amount of expenditure induced by a change in income equals $\Delta E_i/\Delta Y \cdot \Delta Y$, the size of the term $\Delta E_i/\Delta Y$—called the *marginal propensity to spend*—determines the magnitude of the multiplier.

c. The magnitude of the multiplier is equal to one divided by one minus the marginal propensity to spend. Letting K represent the multiplier,

$$K = \frac{1}{1 - \dfrac{\Delta E_i}{\Delta Y}}$$

4   Graph of Income Change

a. In Figure 4.1 EE represents the original planned aggregate expenditure line, producing an equilibrium income level of OY_e. An autonomous increase in planned expenditure is shown by the upward movement of EE to $E'E'$. Accordingly, the equilibrium level of income increases to OY_e', where the new level of aggregate demand equals aggregate supply.

   The multiplier effect shows up in the excess of the increase in income (DC) over the increase in autonomous expenditure (AB). Since $DC = AC$, the excess of DC over $AB = BC$. Hence, BC is the amount of *induced* expenditure. DC (or ΔY) is therefore composed of AB (or ΔE_A) plus BC (or ΔE_i).

b. BC/DC is the *slope* of the expenditure line, and measures the marginal propensity to spend, $\Delta E_i/\Delta Y$. The amount of induced expenditure (BC) is equal to $BC/DC \times DC$, or the marginal propensity to spend multiplied by the change in income.

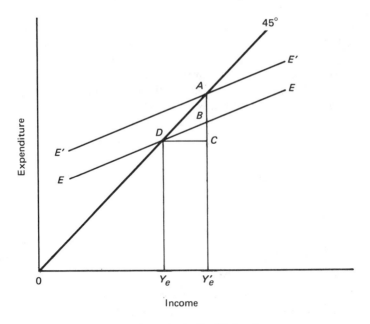

FIGURE 4.1   Change in the Equilibrium Income

B   CONCEPTS

1   Leakages, Injections, and Equilibrium

These concepts appear in Chapter 3. If you are unsure of their meaning, review the previous chapter.

2   Autonomous and Induced Expenditure

a. *Autonomous* expenditures occur independently of the level of income. Causes of autonomous shifts in expenditure include such variables as population growth, technological developments, changes in consumer preferences, changes in interest rates, wars, etc.

b. *Induced* expenditures are those directly dependent upon and related to income. Changes in induced expenditure do not occur *except* in response to *prior* changes in income.

c. All components of aggregate expenditure—consumption, investment, government, and the foreign trade balance—are subject to both autonomous and induced changes. However, investment expenditure and government purchases are the most prone to autonomous shifts. Consumption expenditure *may* change autonomously because of anticipated future shortages or price increases or because of changed attitudes toward saving. Normally, over fairly short periods of time, consumption expenditure maintains a stable relationship with disposable personal income, changing significantly only in response to prior changes in income. The same is true of the *import* component of the foreign trade balance; the *export* component is more closely related to foreign income levels.

3 The Marginal Propensity to Spend

a. The marginal propensity to spend, $\Delta E_i / \Delta Y$, is the ratio of the change in *induced* expenditures to the change in income causing the induced expenditures. For example, if, as a result of an increase in national income by $100, induced expenditures increased by $80, the marginal propensity to spend would be 8/10.

b. The marginal propensity to spend is the *sum* of the marginal propensity to consume the national income, $\Delta C / \Delta Y$; the marginal propensity to invest, $\Delta I / \Delta Y$; the marginal rate of government purchases, $\Delta G / \Delta Y$; and marginal rate of change in the foreign trade balance, $\Delta (X - M)/\Delta Y$:

$$\frac{\Delta E_i}{\Delta Y} = \frac{\Delta C}{\Delta Y} + \frac{\Delta I}{\Delta Y} + \frac{\Delta G}{\Delta Y} + \frac{\Delta (X - M)}{\Delta Y}$$

While $\Delta C / \Delta Y$ normally has a high value, the other propensities usually have relatively low values. It is frequently assumed for analytical purposes that only $\Delta C / \Delta Y$ is greater than zero, in which case $\Delta E_i / \Delta Y = \Delta C / \Delta Y$.

4 The Multiplier

a. Since the multiplier effect is attributable to induced expenditures, the magnitude of the multiplier is determined by the marginal propensity to spend, $\Delta E_i / \Delta Y$, which is the ratio of induced expenditures to income changes.

The multiplier (K) is equal to the reciprocal of one minus the marginal propensity to spend:

$$K = \frac{1}{1 - \dfrac{\Delta E_i}{\Delta Y}}$$

How this formula is derived can be seen by recalling the following relationship:

1682442

$$\Delta Y = \Delta E_A + \frac{\Delta E_i}{\Delta Y} \cdot \Delta Y$$

As explained previously, this states that the ultimate change in income (ΔY) initiated by a change in autonomous expenditure (ΔE_A) is equal to the change in autonomous expenditure, plus the additional expenditure induced by the change in income ($\Delta E_i / \Delta Y \times \Delta Y$). Factoring ΔY in the above equation, we obtain

$$\Delta Y \left(1 - \frac{\Delta E_i}{\Delta Y} \right) = \Delta E_A$$

so that

$$\Delta Y = \Delta E_A \cdot \frac{1}{1 - \dfrac{\Delta E_i}{\Delta Y}}$$

The multiplier is thus equal to the second expression on the right-hand side,

$$\frac{1}{1 - \dfrac{\Delta E_i}{\Delta Y}}$$

or the reciprocal of one minus the marginal propensity to spend.

An example will serve to clarify the basis for the multiplier. Suppose that an autonomous increase in expenditure of $100 occurs. The immediate effect is to increase the national income by $100. The multiplier now takes over. The initial increase in income of $100 in turn induces additional expenditure by an amount equal to $100 times the marginal propensity to spend. For illustrative purposes, let $\Delta E_i / \Delta Y = 1/2$. Then induced expenditure is $100 \times 1/2 = 50. But the induced expenditure constitutes an equivalent further increase in income, which in turn induces another round of induced expenditure, this time of $25 (equal to $50 \times 1/2$). The process continues, with the total cumulative change in income approaching the sum of the series

$$100 + 50 + 25 + 12.5 + \ldots .$$

This series can be expressed as

$$100 + 100 \; \frac{1}{2} + 100 \; \frac{1}{2}^{\,2} + 100 \; \frac{1}{2}^{\,3} + \ldots .$$

The sum of such a geometric series is

$$100 \; \frac{1}{3/2} = 100 \times 2 = 200$$

Hence, the national income ultimately increases by \$200 in response to the initial increase in autonomous expenditure of \$100. The other \$100 of income consists of the sum of induced expenditure. The multiplier in this case is 2, equal to the bracketed expression above—the reciprocal of one minus the marginal propensity to spend—the formula for the multiplier.

A summary in tabular form of this example is:

Autonomous Expenditure	Induced Expenditure	Total Cumulative Expenditure
	$\dfrac{\Delta E_i}{\Delta Y} = \dfrac{1}{2}$	$(=Y)$
100	—	100
—	50	150
—	25	175
—	12.5	187.5
—	6.25	193.75
Limit Approached:	100	200

b. As indicated previously, the most important type of induced expenditure is *consumption* expenditure. As a first approximation, it is sometimes assumed that consumption is the only induced expenditure item, with the other components of the national income assumed to be entirely autonomous. In this case, the marginal propensity to spend is the same as the marginal propensity to consume the national income, $\Delta C / \Delta Y$, and the multiplier formula reduces to

$$K = \frac{1}{1 - \dfrac{\Delta C}{\Delta Y}}$$

The multiplier formula becomes more complicated if account is taken of taxes, as must be done if the relationship is to have any empirical significance. The consumption function relates consumption to disposable personal income rather than to the national income. If, for simplicity, we exclude business corporations, personal income is identical to national income, and disposable personal income (DPY) is equal to the national income, minus taxes (T):

$$DPY = Y - T$$

But taxes are not given independently of the national income. With given tax rates, the total tax yield varies directly with the national income. This can be expressed as

$$T = tY,$$

where t is $\Delta T/\Delta Y$, or the marginal rate of taxation.

Substituting this tax function into the equation of disposable personal income, we have

$$DPY = Y - tY = Y(1-t)$$

Now let us assume that investment expenditure, government expenditure, and the trade balance are all autonomous, totaling an amount we shall call A. This leaves only consumption as an induced expenditure, equal to the national income multiplied by the marginal propensity to consume. Letting c represent $\Delta C/\Delta(DPY)$, or the marginal propensity to consume, we obtain the following expression for the equilibrium national income:

$$Y = c(Y-tY) + A$$

This is an equilibrium equation, for Y is output or aggregate supply, and the right-hand side represents aggregate demand.

The above equation can be rewritten as

$$Y(1 - c+ct) = A$$

so that

$$Y = A \times \frac{1}{1 - c + ct} = A \times \frac{1}{1 - c(1-t)}.$$

By using calculus, it can be shown that this leads to the following:

$$\frac{\Delta Y}{\Delta A} = \frac{1}{1 - c(1-t)}$$

where the right-hand side is the multiplier.

Hence, the result is fairly simple: with taxes introduced into the picture, the multiplier K is equal to the reciprocal of one minus the marginal propensity to consume multiplied by one minus the marginal rate of taxation:

$$K = \frac{1}{1 - c(1-t)}$$

C   DISCUSSION

1   The Roles of Autonomous and Induced Expenditure

All expenditure on currently produced goods and services, whether autonomous or induced expenditure, contributes to the national income. Nevertheless, the difference between autonomous and induced expenditure is vital for the explanation of changes in income.

Induced expenditure cannot account for any movement in income away from an initial equilibrium level. For such a movement to begin, there must be a shift in autonomous expenditure. Once this occurs, the produced change in income leads to induced changes in expenditure.

Investment expenditure and government purchases—the primary types of autonomous expenditure—typically initiate movements in income. A technological advance opening up profitable investment opportunities, an expected increase in business sales leading to increased inventories, an acceleration of family formation causing the demand for housing to increase—all these are examples of reasons for an autonomous increase in investment expenditure.

Examples of reasons for autonomous increases in government purchases include deterioration in international relations causing military expenditures to rise and enlargement of the public sector of the economy for schools, highways, slum clearance, pollution control.

2   Self-Feeding Income Changes: The Multiplier Effects

Any movement in national income tends to generate further movements in the same direction; the phenomenon is the *multiplier effect.*

Changes in spending, induced whenever an initial change in income occurs, provide underlying causes of the self-feeding movement in income. Suppose that an autonomous increase in investment expenditure raises income by an equal amount. This in turn induces an increase in consumption spending, which contributes equivalently to a further increase in income.

The self-generating process of income changes does not continue indefinitely. Indeed, at successive rounds of income-expenditure, the self-generating forces diminish in strength because income changes induce not only additional spending but additional tax liabilities and saving. Tax and saving *leakages* operate to keep expenditure amounts smaller than the increase in income inducing the expenditure. The leakages become cumulatively greater until they approach in total amount the autonomous *injections* which initiated the income movement. At this point, income is at a new equilibrium level, without further change occurring.

D CONFUSIONS TO AVOID

1 The Propensity to Consume and the Propensity to Spend

Consumption is always the single largest expenditure item in the national income and, correspondingly, the largest contributor to the marginal propensity to spend. However, the marginal propensities to consume and to spend are not equal to each other, except under highly restrictive assumptions. For the two propensities to be equal, these conditions are necessary:

a. No expenditure item other than consumption is subject to induced changes. This is equivalent to saying that investment expenditure, government purchases, and the foreign trade balance are completely autonomous and immune to change as a result of income changes. If these conditions hold, then the marginal propensity to spend ($\Delta E_i / \Delta Y$) is equal to the marginal propensity to consume the national income ($\Delta C / \Delta Y$).

b. Any change in income must be accompanied by an equivalent change in disposable personal income. This is necessary because the marginal propensity to consume the national income relates changes in consumption expenditure to changes in the national income ($\Delta C / \Delta Y$), while the marginal propensity to consume relates changes in consumption expenditure to changes in disposable personal income ($\Delta C / \Delta DPY$).

The national income and disposable personal income are equal only if there are no taxes and transfer payments and no business saving. Correspondingly, $\Delta C / \Delta Y = \Delta C / \Delta DPY$ only if no portion of any change in national income is absorbed by changes in taxes or changes in business saving.

In reality, this could never be true. But the violence to reality can be greatly reduced if the impact of tax changes is taken into account even though changes in business saving continue to be ignored. This is commonly done in textbook presentations by the formula

$$\frac{\Delta C}{\Delta Y} = \frac{\Delta C}{\Delta DPY} (1 - \frac{\Delta T}{\Delta Y})$$

CHAPTER 5 UNEMPLOYMENT AND INFLATION

A PRINCIPLES

1 Unemployment

Employment opportunities depend upon the level of the real national income. The cause of *general unemployment* is too low a level of national income, or deficient aggregate demand for goods and services.

Unemployment occurring in particular occupations or regions because of a structural imbalance is called *structural unemployment.*

2 Inflation

a. *Demand-pull inflation* is the result of a too-rapidly expanding money national income, or excessive aggregate demand.

b. *Cost-push inflation* is caused by increases in average and marginal costs of production, largely attributable to more rapid increases in wage rates than in labor productivity.

3 Deflationary and Inflationary Gaps

a. The amount by which aggregate demand is below the volume required for full employment is called the *deflationary gap.* The deflationary gap is equal to the excess of the full-employment level of taxes plus planned saving over the sum of the current levels of planned investment, government expenditure, and the foreign trade balance.

   b. The amount by which aggregate demand exceeds the volume required for full employment is the *inflationary gap*. The inflationary gap is equal to the excess of the sum of current planned investment, government expenditure, and the foreign trade balance over the full-employment level of taxes plus planned saving.

B   CONCEPTS

1   Definition of Unemployment and Full Employment

   A person is unemployed if he is able, willing, and seeking employment, but cannot find a job. Those persons not looking for employment, or not able or willing to work, or engaged outside the market labor force (e.g., housewives) are not regarded as unemployed.

   It is impossible for every member of the labor force to be continuously employed. At any moment there will be a certain number of people who are in between jobs. This is known as "frictional" unemployment. In the United States, 3 to 4 percent frictional unemployment of the labor force is considered unavoidable. Hence, "full employment" is said to exist when unemployment does not exceed the unavoidable minimum of 3 to 4 percent of the labor force.

   Structural unemployment is that attributable not to a lack of job opportunities but rather to a lack of required training or skills, unwillingness or inability to move to another location, etc.

2   Meaning of Inflation

   Inflation means an increase in the average level of prices of goods and services. The prices of some goods and services may rise without causing inflation if the prices of other goods and services fall and so restore the balance.

   The average level of prices must be weighted in accordance with the relative importance of the goods and services in the national income. Such a weighted average is found in price indexes published periodically by the United States Bureau of Labor Statistics.

   Demand-pull inflation connotes a rise in the average level of prices resulting from too great a demand for goods and services. *Cost-push inflation* refers to a rise in the average level of prices stemming from the supply side, with particular reference to increased costs.

3   Deflationary and Inflationary Gaps

   The reference base for identifying deflationary and inflationary gaps is the *full-employment national income,* defined as that level of national income which would be produced with full employment of resources.

Realizing the full-employment national income requires a certain amount of *aggregate planned expenditure.* If this expenditure is less than the required amount, the short-fall is a measure of a deflationary gap; if actual planned expenditure is greater than the amount required for full employment, the excess is a measure of an inflationary gap. A graphic representation of the gaps is shown in Figure 5.1.

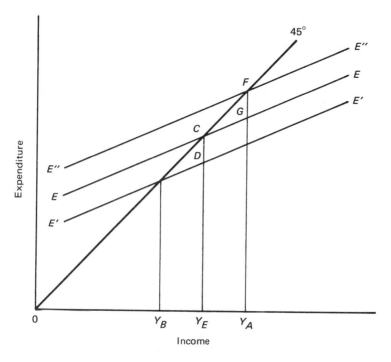

FIGURE 5.1 Deflationary and Inflationary Gaps

In the figure, Y_E is the full–employment level of national income. This level will tend to prevail as the equilibrium income if the aggregate planned expenditure line is *EE.* If in fact the planned expenditure line is $E'E'$, the equilibrium level of income is Y_B and unemployment occurs. The vertical distance between the *EE* and $E'E'$ lines (CD) is a deflationary gap. On the other hand, if planned expenditure is $E''E''$, the equilibrium income is Y_A and there is an inflationary gap equal to *FG.*

An alternative method of identifying inflationary and deflationary gaps is in terms of injections and leakages. The national income tends to settle at the level where injections and leakages are equal. Hence, income will tend to the full-employment level if the volume of leakages at that income level is matched by the volume of injections. If injections are less than full-employment leakages, a deflationary gap prevails; if injections exceed full-employment leakages, an inflationary gap exists.

Given tax rates and the saving function, full-employment leakages consist of the taxes collected (T_f) and the planned saving desired (S_f) when the national income is at the full-employment level. Injections consist of planned investment (I_p), government expenditure (G), and the foreign trade balance $(X-M)$. Hence, if

$$T_f + S_f > I_p + G + (X-M),$$

there is a deflationary gap equal to the excess of the left side over the right side of the inequality. If, on the other hand,

$$T_f + S_f < I_p + G + (X-M),$$

there is an inflationary gap equal to the excess of the right side over the left side of the inequality.

C DISCUSSION

1 Income and Employment

a. The dependence of employment opportunities upon real income is obvious upon reflection. The real national income is the nation's output of goods and services. Producing these goods and services requires the employment of productive agents. Given the quality and quantity of productive resources and the state of technology, the real national income will be at a certain level with full employment. If it is less than this it must mean that not all productive resources are fully employed. Hence, to have full employment, aggregate demand must be great enough to lead to an equilibrium level of national income which requires the full use of productive resources.

b. Even when the national income is at the full-employment level, there will be *structural* unemployment because of the mismatching of jobs and the resources available to do them. For example, there may be a need and demand for computer programmers in excess of the number of workers trained in this area. Characteristic of such structural unemployment is the coexistence of unfilled jobs and unemployment.

It is clear that while ordinary unemployment can be eliminated by an expansion of national income, the cure for structural unemployment lies elsewhere—in training programs, more education, etc.

2 Income and Inflation

a. While too small an aggregate demand leads to unemployment, too great a demand leads to inflation. Demand is "too great" when it cannot be satisfied. If in the aggregate, consumers, businesses, and government wish to purchase more goods and services than are available, the inevitable consequence is a general bidding up of prices.

The full-employment output of an economy represents the maximum current supply of goods and services. If aggregate planned expenditure is greater than this full-employment supply, the excess of demand over supply forces prices upward. This situation contrasts with that of unemployment where an excess of aggregate demand over current supply simply leads to an expansion of supply through the employment of idle resources. Instead of prices being bid up, more resources are employed.

b. Just as there may be structural unemployment even when national income is at the full-employment level, so there may be inflation when national income is below the full-employment level. In this case, however, the inflation is clearly not due to excess demand (demand–pull inflation), but rather to cost–push forces.

The most common cause of cost increases is wage increments in excess of productivity increases. Wage costs per unit of output equal wage rates divided by the output per worker. If wage rates rise more rapidly than output per worker, wage costs per unit of output increase. Business firms respond sooner or later by increasing the prices of their products.

While demand–pull inflation can be cured by reducing aggregate expenditure, the remedy for cost–push inflation consists of measures to keep wage rates and labor productivity in line with each other.

D CONFUSIONS TO AVOID

1 Deflationary and Inflationary Gaps

Care should be exercised in distinguishing between the deflationary and inflationary gaps, on the one hand, and the deficiency, or excess of national income below or above the full-employment level, on the other.

Suppose that the noninflationary, full-employment national income for a given year is $875 billion, while the actual level of income for that year is $850 billion. The national income is thus $25 billion short of full employment. But this is not the amount of the deflationary gap, for an increase in planned expenditure of less than $25 billion would cause the national income to rise by $25 billion, owing to the *multiplier* effect. If the multiplier is two, for example, an increase in planned expenditure of $12.5 billion would raise the national income by $25 billion. The deflationary gap therefore is $12.5 billion. The same point applies to the inflationary gap.

CHAPTER 6   FLUCTUATIONS IN INCOME, EMPLOYMENT, AND PRICES

A   PRINCIPLES

1   Cyclical Fluctuations

There is an inherent tendency for the national income to fluctuate around the long-run, or secular, trend. This is known as *cyclical fluctuations,* or the *business cycle.*

   a. When the national income is above the long-run trend and is rising, the economy is in the *expansion,* or *prosperity,* phase of the cycle.

   b. When the national income is falling or is below the trend, the economy is in the *contraction,* or *recession,* phase of the cycle.

   c. The point of the cycle at which an expansion stage ends and gives way to contraction is called the *upper turning point;* the end of contraction and beginning of expansion is at the *lower turning point* of the cycle.

2   The Main Cause of Fluctuations

The general cause of cyclical fluctuations is changes in *investment expenditure.* Investment fluctuates in response to "external" (or exogenous) disturbances—such as technological advances, population growth, political disturbances—and "internal" (or endogenous) forces—such as monetary conditions, rate of sales, expectations, cost and availability of labor and materials.

3   The Acceleration Principle

A major contributing factor to fluctuations in economic activity is the *acceleration effect.* The principle involved is that fluctuations in sales become magnified into larger fluctuations in investment. As income and sales rise in a recovery period, plant, equipment, and inventories investment rise by a larger percentage amount. As income and sales begin to level off or increase at a decreasing rate in the later stage of prosperity, investment decreases.

Interacting with the multiplier, the *accelerator* helps to explain the momentum of the recovery and contraction phases of the business cycle as well as its upper and lower turning points.

4   Turning Points

a. The eventual termination of prosperity is normally brought about by a combination of forces. Among these are usually found:

1. the gradual exhaustion of profitable investment opportunities,
2. decreasing efficiency and rising costs as capacity is approached, and
3. expectations of a forthcoming contraction.

b. The eventual recovery from a recession is typically associated with:

1. the need to replace depleted plant and equipment and inventories,
2. new investment opportunities created by technological advances,
3. lower costs because of the ready availability of labor, materials, and credit, and
4. expectations of recovery.

B   CONCEPTS

1   Trend and Cycle

A time series showing the level of economic activity in the United States over, say, a 50-year period displays a very uneven movement. In some years the level of activity (as measured by an index of production or employment, for example) will be shown rising, in other years falling. The long-run trend is a kind of average of these ups and downs. When plotted on a graph, as in Figure 6.1, the trend appears as a smooth, upward-sloping line. *Cylical fluctuations* appear as the vertical deviations above and below the trend line.

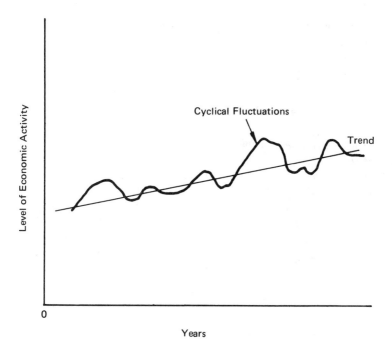

FIGURE 6.1 The Business Cycle

2 Phases of the Cycle

a. *Prosperity* (sometimes called "boom" or cyclical "peak") is characterized by a declining rate of unemployment and a tendency for wages
and prices to rise.

b. *Recession* (the older term "depression" is used for a severe and prolonged
recession) is characterized by a rising rate of unemployment and idle
resources. Wages and prices tend to be stable, though in a severe recession they may actually decline (deflation).

c. The *upper turning point* is characterized by a leveling off of economic
activity, with a slowing down, or cessation, of previous rates of growth
in production, employment, and prices.

d. The *lower turning point* is characterized by the beginning of an upturn
in production and employment.

3 External and Internal Disturbances

An *external* (*exogenous*) disturbance to the economy arises outside the economic structure and is independent of the operation of the economic mechanism.

An *internal* (endogenous) distrubance originates within the economic system itself and is a consequence of the workings of the system.

4 The Acceleration Principle

The *acceleration principle* can best be explained by an example. Suppose that a firm, to operate in its usual way, maintains a ratio of 5 to 1 between its plant and equipment and its annual output. At the start, assume that the firm's annual sales (output) are $100 and its plant and equipment are worth $500. As long as sales remain at $100 per year, no new plant and equipment is required, but the replacement of used-up equipment is necessary, say at the rate of 10 percent, or $50, per year. In this case, *net* investment is zero, *gross* investment is $50.

Now let sales increase by 10 percent—from $100 to $110. To maintain the capital-output ratio of 5 to 1, an addition to plant and equipment of $50 is necessary. Hence, *net* investment is $50, but the replacement of $50 of old equipment continues as before, making *gross* investment $100. The 10 percent increase in sales and output has led to a 100 percent increase in gross investment.

Next, suppose that while sales continue to rise, the *rate* of increase falls— say from $110 to $115, or an increase of less than 5 percent. Net investment of $25 (to bring plant and equipment to $575), plus replacement investment of $50, makes gross investment $75, or a decrease of 25 percent over the previous year.

These hypothetical data, together with other assumed changes in sales and output with their impact on gross investment, are summarized in the following table:

Year	Sales	Required Plant and Equipment	Replacement Investment	Net Investment	Gross Investment
1	$100	$500	$ $50	$ 0	$ 50
2	110	550	50	50	100
3	115	575	50	25	75
4	115	575	50	0	50
5	110	550	0	0	0

For gross investment merely to remain constant, sales and output must continue to rise each year. Any slowing down in the rate of increase in sales causes investment to decline, and if sales actually drop in volume, gross investment falls to zero.

C   DISCUSSION

1   The Inherent Tendency Toward Income Fluctuations

The national income changes whenever it is in disequilibrium—*i.e.*, when planned saving and taxes (leakages) do not equal planned investment, government purchases, and the foreign trade balance (injections).

Inequality of leakages and injections is the *norm.* This is because different decision-makers with different motives are responsible for leakages and injections. Just because, for example, some firms and households may decide to make larger investment expenditure, there is no reason to expect other firms and households to decide simultaneously to save a larger fraction of their income, or for the government to raise tax rates.

2   The Special Role of Investment

Investment expenditure is the most volatile component of the national income. More than any other type of expenditure, investment is susceptible to the autonomous shifts which initiate movements in income. In addition, it is subject to induced changes as expressed in the acceleration principle.

Several factors account for the great sensitivity of investment. Investments inherently involve time and the future, with returns spread out over months or years. Since some degree of uncertainty is inescapable, decisions are increasingly sensitive to a wide variety of forces affecting the future of the economy. Moreover, unlike the greatest part of consumption expenditure and government purchases, investment is generally postponable. (This is also true of expenditure on durable consumer goods, purchases of which fluctuate much more widely than nondurable consumer goods.) The ability to postpone replacement of and additions to plant and equipment, housing, and inventories widens the degree of freedom in the timing of investment decisions.

3   Why Prosperity (and Recession) Eventually End

Historically, every period of expansion in income and employment has at some point ended and given way to contraction. The same is true, in reverse, for every period of contraction. This is the essence of the business cycle.

Why does the income movement in a given direction continue indefinitely? Because the requirements are usually too demanding to be realizable. Consider an expansion phase: for income and employment to continue to expand, in each succeeding year injections into the income-expenditure stream must exceed the leakages. In a nonregulated economy, this means that planned private investment expenditure must continue to increase year after year. (The extent to which deficiencies in private investment can be compensated by government measures will be examined in the next chapter.) This in turn would require that, on balance, the numerous external and internal influences on investment decisions always be expansionist—a highly improbably contingency.

Even stronger tendencies rule out the indefinite continuance of a contraction in income and employment: as income falls, the amount of planned saving and tax leakages decreases (as it increases when income rises). The amount of injections required to compensate for the leakages thus decreases. Moreover, injections cannot continue to decrease forever. Plant and equipment wear out, housing deteriorates, and inventories become depleted. At some point replacement and replenishment become necessary to maintain even a low level of output. And, inevitably, sooner or later some shock to the system, such as a technological breakthrough, triggers an upward movement in income.

D   CONFUSIONS TO AVOID

1   The Difference Between the Multiplier and the Accelerator

The multiplier and the accelerator interact with each other to give impetus to any given movement in income; but the two effects are produced differently and can be distinguished analytically.

The multiplier effect (see Chapter 4) is the result of induced changes in *consumption* expenditure. The accelerator effect is the result of induced changes in *investment* expenditure. Both effects are normally set off by a prior change in income.

2   Implications of the Business "Cycle"

The word "cycle" should not convey the impression that fluctuations in economic activity fall neatly into a regular pattern. While there are certain characteristics of different cycles, each has unique features. Thus, even though we can be fairly confident that a prosperity period will be followed by recession, and vice-versa, the duration and amplitude of fluctuations vary widely from cycle to cycle.

CHAPTER 7

COUNTERCYCLICAL FISCAL POLICY FOR
FULL EMPLOYMENT AND PRICE STABILITY

A PRINCIPLES

1 Meaning of Countercyclical Fiscal Policy

Countercyclical fiscal policy refers to the discretionary or planned *expenditure* and *taxation* actions of the government (chiefly at the federal level) for the purpose of controlling aggregate spending in the economy.

2 Objectives of Countercyclical Fiscal Policy

The chief objectives of modern fiscal policy are to promote *full employment* and *price stability.* Stated conversely, the objectives are to minimize *unemployment* and *inflation.*

3 The Influence of Government Expenditure and Taxes on the National Income

a. Government purchases of goods and services are *injections* into the income–expenditure stream. Other things being equal, the larger government spending is, the greater the national income.

b. Taxes are *leakages* from the income–expenditure stream. Other things being equal, the higher the tax rates, the smaller the national income.

c. *Equal* increases in taxes and in government purchases normally have a net *expansionary* effect on the national income. This is called the *balanced–budget multiplier theorem.*

d. High levels of government spending and high and progressive tax rates exert a general *stabilizing* influence on the national income. Other important *built-in stabilizers* are transfer payments and unemployment insurance.

4   Fiscal Instruments

a. In periods of threatened or actual recession and unemployment, government fiscal policy will shift to either an increase in purchases of goods and services or a decrease in tax rates, or both.

b. In periods of threatened or actual inflation, government fiscal policy tends to either reduce government spending or increase tax rates, or both.

5   Budgetary and Debt Implications of Fiscal Policy

a. If the government's budget is currently balanced (expenditures equal to receipts), a fiscal policy then undertaken to restore full employment in a period of unemployment leads to a *budget deficit* and an increase in the national debt. With a balanced budget, a fiscal policy shift to overcome inflation leads to a *budget surplus* and a reduction in the national debt.

b. The doctrine that the government should seek to keep its budget balanced at all times is therefore inconsistent with fiscal policy for full employment and stability.

Often expressed opinions that budget deficits are necessarily inflationary, that a large public debt may threaten the economy with bankruptcy, or that deficit financing allows the burden of the deficit to accrue to future generations, are not generally accepted as valid by economists.

B   CONCEPTS

1   Countercyclical Fiscal Policy

Government expenditure and taxation have several aspects and objectives. The most general purpose of government expenditure is to provide "public" goods and services—*i.e.,* goods and services not provided adequately by private producers. The most general purpose of taxation is to gain the revenue for financing the production and purchase of public goods and services. Changing the market distribution of personal income becomes an important ancillary purpose of taxation.

The various questions and issues raised by these fundamental objectives of fiscal policy are presented in Chapter 20.

Countercyclical fiscal policy is oriented quite differently. It is not directed at considerations such as the proper allocation of resources between private and public sectors, or the most equitable distribution of tax burdens, even though these may be indirectly affected. Rather, countercyclical fiscal policy aims at controlling the overall level of aggregate spending in the economy. Consequently, the primary factor becomes the amount and timing of *changes* in government expenditure and tax rates. Expenditures are increased or decreased in order to change aggregate demand and thus avoid unemployment or inflation. Tax rates are changed not for the purpose of providing more or less revenue *per se,* but to influence private expenditure.

2   Full Employment and Price Stability

Full employment is defined as a rate of unemployment of the labor force no greater than 3 to 4 percent. Price stability means the absence of increases in the weighted average level of prices, as measured by a general price index. (For a fuller description of these terms, see Chapter 5.)

3   Injections and Leakages

Injections into the income-expenditure stream consist of planned investment expenditure, government purchases of goods and services, and the foreign trade balance. Leakages from the income–expenditure stream consist of planned saving and taxes. (For a broader statement of these terms, see Chapter 3.)

4   Built-In Stabilizers

These refer to the forces in the economy that automatically operate to restrain fluctuations in the national income; prime examples are the federal individual income tax and unemployment insurance programs.

When the national income rises, income tax payments increase because of higher tax bases and movement into higher tax brackets. As a result, *disposable* income rises by a smaller amount than the increase in national income, thus restraining the increment in induced expenditure. When the national income falls, the reverse occurs: disposable income falls by a smaller amount, restraining the reduction in induced expenditure.

Unemployment insurance works in the same way. In periods of unemployment, personal income is sustained by unemployment compensation; in periods of full employment, insurance payments keep disposable income lower than it would be otherwise.

5　The Government's National Income Budget

All government expenditures for goods and services are included as part of the national income. Government spending for other purposes–such as for social security, subsidies, pensions, etc.–are not included in the national income, since they are *transfer payments* and do not represent expenditure on currently produced goods and services. Interest on the national debt is also regarded as a transfer payment.

All tax payments to the government are counted in calculating the tax leakage from the income–expenditure flow, whether or not they are included in the government's regular operating budget (the so-called "administrative budget"). For example, payroll taxes under Social Security are not part of the administrative budget, but accounted for, as are social security payments, in separate "trust funds."

The budget which is relevant to the national income is called the *national income budget.*

C　DISCUSSION

1　The Role of Government Spending in the National Income

Government spending on goods and services (G) is one of the components of the national income equation or identity (review Chapter 2 to refresh your memory on this point):

$$Y = C + I + G + (X - M)$$

Government expenditure is no different in this respect from consumption or either of the other components of income. One dollar spent by the government on currently produced goods or services directly contributes a dollar to the national income.

Moreover, like any other national income spending, government expenditure is responsible indirectly for additional income through the multiplier effect.

Suppose the government increases its spending by $1 billion. Accordingly, the national income rises by this amount which in turn induces an increase in consumption expenditure (and perhaps also in investment expenditure). The final total impact on the national income is found by multiplying the $1 billion by the multiplier. If the multiplier is 2, for instance, the national income tends to rise by $2 billion as a consequence of the increase in government purchases of $1 billion.

2   The Role of Taxes in the National Income

While government spending accelerates the national income, taxes serve as a brake. The higher the national income is, the greater the tax revenue produced by given tax rates. But the greater the tax rates, the smaller the national income (other things remaining equal) because tax payments reduce business and personal disposable income, cutting down private spending.

An increase in taxes at a given level of national income therefore reduces the national income by contracting private expenditure. A $1 billion increase in tax rates tends to reduce private spending initially by less than $1 billion, for part of the reduction in disposable income is accounted for by reduced planned saving. Suppose that the marginal propensity to save is 1/10 and the 9/10 left is the marginal propensity to consume. If a tax increase of $1 reduces disposable personal income by a similar amount, consumption expenditure falls by 9/10 × $1 = $0.90. However, the national income decreases by $0.90 times the multiplier. If the multiplier is 2, the $1 increase in taxes causes the national income to decrease by $1.80.

This can now be stated in more formal terms. Letting T represent a change in taxes, c the marginal propensity to consume, and t the marginal rate of taxation:

$$\Delta Y = -\Delta T \ \frac{c}{1-c(1-t)}$$

The right-hand side of this equation is equal to the change in consumption caused by the tax change $(\Delta T \cdot c)$ times the multiplier $[1/1-c\,(1-t)]$.

3   The Balanced-Budget Multiplier

If government spending and taxes are increased or decreased by the same amount—leaving the budget balance unaffected—what will be the effects on the national income? The prediction is that the national income will undergo a net change in the same direction as the change in government expenditure and taxes. The reason for this is that the impact on income of a dollar's change in government spending is greater than the impact of a dollar's change in taxes. All of government's extra expenditure generates income, while only part of extra taxes affect expenditure, since the remainder affects planned saving. Thus, assuming a multiplier of 2 and a marginal propensity to consume of 8/10, an extra dollar of government expenditure causes income to expand by $2, while an extra dollar of taxes causes income to fall by only $1.60 (that is, 8/10 of $1 times 2). More formally stated:

$$\Delta Y = \Delta G \cdot \frac{1}{1-c(1-t)}$$

and

$$\Delta Y = -\Delta T \cdot \frac{c}{1-c(1-t)}$$

If $\Delta G = \Delta T$, the positive change in income from ΔG would equal the negative change from ΔT only if the marginal propensity to consume (c) equals 1. Since c is usually less than 1, the positive effect of ΔG is greater than the negative effect of ΔT.

4 Fiscal Instruments

a. To eliminate *unemployment* (nonstructural), additional spending on goods and services is required. The required amount of extra spending is measured in terms of the *deflationary gap* (see Chapter 5).

   The government can use either of two methods, or a combination of both, to increase total spending: it can increase its *own* spending, or, by lowering tax rates, it can encourage an increase in *private* spending. To state this proposition in a slightly different way: to eliminate a deflationary gap, the government can either directly increase injections into the income–expenditure stream, or reduce leakages from the income–expenditure stream (see Chapter 3).

   It should be noted that an increase in government expenditure is likely to have a greater impact on the national income than would an equivalent decrease in taxes, for the reasons given previously in this section. However, there may be other reasons for preferring tax changes to government spending, such as political feasibility, quicker action by the Congress, and the impact on the proportion of the public sector to the private sector.

b. To eliminate *inflation* (demand–pull), a reduction in aggregate spending on goods and services is required. The government can reduce its own expenditure or encourage a reduction in private spending by increasing tax rates, or both. In other words, an *inflationary gap* can be closed by reducing injections or increasing leakages in the income-expenditure stream.

5 Fiscal Policy and the National Debt

a. To the extent that government spending exceeds tax revenue, *borrowing* is necessary; this increases the *national debt.*

b. Unless the government's budget is in a *surplus* position initially— with tax revenues in excess of spending—a fiscal policy to eliminate unemployment creates a, or adds to an existing, budget *deficit* and increases the national debt. Unless the budget is in a deficit position initially, fiscal policy to eliminate inflation creates a, or adds to an existing, budgetary surplus, which may be used to reduce the national debt.

c. Deficit financing and an accompanying increase in the national debt is not necessarily inflationary, a threat to national solvency, nor a device to shift financial burdens to future generations.

Inflation is caused by excessive aggregate demand. Changes in fiscal policy in such a case work toward a budgetary surplus and a reduction in the national debt. If there is unemployment, deficit financing contributes to fuller employment rather than to inflation, even though inflation tends to build up as full employment is approached.

The national debt does not lead to national bankruptcy. Unlike individuals and private business firms, the government has the power to tax and therefore is able, except under the most extreme circumstances, to meet any debt obligations. Moreover, the national debt, to the extent that it is internally held, is not a net charge on the national economy: the government's liabilities are matched by assets of those to whom the debt is owed.

Finally, the real burden or cost of government expenditures cannot be shifted to the future, since the burden consists of sacrificed alternatives at the time the expenditures are made.

(NOTE: This is not meant to imply that the national debt has no influence, for it has in a variety of ways—in the management of monetary affairs; in contributing to higher levels of future taxation which may affect the efficiency and growth of the economy; and in affecting the distribution of income. These aspects will be considered at the appropriate points in other chapters.)

D   CONFUSIONS TO AVOID

1   Fiscal Orthodoxy and Countercyclical Fiscal Policies

The view that "sound" budgetary policy calls for keeping the budget in balance—regardless of the state of the overall economy—was once accepted doctrine and still is widely held. This idea was based largely on the observed prudent behavior of individuals and families. But what is true for an individual, family, business firm, or other particular segment of the economy need not be valid for the government. The federal government is the only single participant in the national economy able, by virtue of its size and fiscal powers, to exert a controlling influence on general economic conditions. Exercising such an influence in the direction of economic stability demands a more flexible doctrine than one based on the balanced budget. The common notions that government expenditure should never be increased beyond comparable tax revenue, nor taxes ever changed except in the case of extra expenditures or to match decreased expenditures, are contrary to the tenets of countercyclical policy.

2   Eliminating a Budget Deficit

Fiscal policy measures are rarely without important "feedbacks" which alter the original budgetary impact of the measures. A prime illustration is the feedback of lowered tax rates. If taxes are reduced by, say, $10 billion, the immediate budgetary effect is to increase the government's deficit (or decrease its surplus) by the same amount. But the tax cut will increase the national income and this in turn augments tax collections. The ultimate net result is likely to be a much smaller deficit in the government's budget than was originally created by the tax reduction. Eventually, if the tax cut serves to set off a chain reaction of income expansion in a recovery phase of the business cycle, tax collections will quite possibly reach a larger total under the lower rates than they would have under the original rates.

By the same reasoning, raising tax rates to eliminate a budget deficit, may "backfire" because of the decrease in national income such a measure may entail. (If the economy is suffering from inflation, however, the tax increase may be highly desirable nevertheless.)

CHAPTER **8** THE NATURE AND
SUPPLY OF MONEY

A PRINCIPLES

1 Definition and Functions of Money

a. Money is anything that is generally acceptable at face value for the payment for goods and services and the settlement of debts and other financial transactions.

b. The three standard social functions of money are to serve as a *standard of value,* a *store of value,* and as a *medium of exchange.*

2 Composition of Money Supply

The money supply of modern countries consists of *coins, paper currency,* and *demand deposits* in commercial banks. Demand deposits predominate quantitatively by a wide margin.

3 The Nature of Modern Money

Modern money consists of *debts* of issuing institutions. Coins contain metals of market value, but the market value is usually less than the face, or nominal, value of the coins. Paper currency and demand deposits possess no inherent value as commodities.

4   The Sources of Money Supply

a. Coins in the United States are minted by the United States Treasury Department and paper currency is issued by Federal Reserve Banks *in response to public demand.* Changes in the amount of coins and currency in circulation does not affect the total amount of money in circulation.

b. Bank deposit money is *created* by private commercial banks in the process of their making loans and financial investments. Bank deposit money is *destroyed* by the repayment of bank loans and financial *dis*investment by banks. The economy's supply of bank deposit money therefore increases or decreases according to whether new bank loans and financial investments are greater or less than the repayment of old loans and financial disinvestment.

B   CONCEPTS

1   The Functions of Money

a. A developed economy, with extensive division of labor and specialization, requires some common *standard of value* to express economic values. The established historical monetary standard most commonly consisted of some valuable commodity, principally gold or silver. In the United States today the formal, legal monetary standard is gold. In reality, however, except for international purposes, gold serves as a standard of value only in a nominal sense. For *internal* purposes, the United States is now effectively on a "paper standard," meaning that our standard monetary unit is simply the *dollar,* conceived as an abstract unit and without any specified relationship to any particular commodity. The universal practice in the United States of quoting prices in terms of dollars (and its fractions) is sufficient to validate the dollar as the standard monetary unit.

b. The wealth of a nation does *not* include its stock of money, except to the extent that its money is composed of valuable metals or other commodities. But to the individual owner, money clearly is wealth. Indeed, unless money were available as a *store of wealth,* it would be extremely inconvenient for individuals, business firms, etc. to conduct their economic affairs.

c. The most familiar, and perhaps most basic function of money is to serve as a *medium of exchange.* Without money, exchange of goods and

services—the necessary result of division of labor and specialization—
would have to be on a barter basis. In a monetary economy, goods and
services are exchanged for each other indirectly via the intermediary of
money.

2 The Nature of Bank Deposits

Coins and paper currency are used primarily to transact small retail and
service trade. The great bulk of monetary payments is made with checks written
against bank demand deposits.

Everyone is familiar with coins and paper currency, but bank deposits are
somewhat less understood. First let us summarize what bank deposits are *not.*
They are not coins and paper currency. Of course, coins and paper currency can
be "deposited" in a bank, but this acquired deposit does not itself consist of the
coins and currency, which become the property of the bank. Rather, a bank deposit is a *debt* of the bank owed to the owner of the deposit. The debt is evidenced through entries in the books of the bank and in the passbook of the
owner.

A *demand* deposit, as the name suggests, is a debt of the bank which is pay-
able upon the demand of the owner. This contrasts with *time* and *savings* deposits which are debts that a bank is not obliged to discharge without some form of
advance notice. For this reason, time and savings deposits are not usually included in money supply, but are regarded as "near" money.

The normal way in which a bank discharges its demand deposit liabilities is
by the owners' writing checks against their accounts to make payments to other
people. A second, but quantitatively less important way, is for depositors to
"cash" checks written against their accounts in exchange for receiving coins or
currency from the bank.

It should be noted that when payment is made to someone by a check,
the bank discharges its liability to the maker of the check, but has incurred a
debt to the payee of the check. In other words, payment by check merely trans-
fers the liability of the bank from one person to another.

Since bank deposits are debts or liabilities of the bank, they appear in the
liability column of the bank's "T-account." A T-account is a statement of assets
and liabilities; conventionally, the assets are listed on the left side of a vertical
line while the liabilities are listed on the right side. If $1000 in currency is de-
posited in a bank, the T-account of the bank would show the following entries:

Assets	*Liabilities*
Currency $1000	Deposits $1000

C DISCUSSION

1 Meaning and Nature of Money

One might say that "money is what money does." Anything that is generally acceptable in making payments can be called money. It is not surprising that the earliest forms of money were commodities having a market value; this value was necessary for their general acceptability. Coming with the development of more sophisticated institutions and ideas, however, was the trend of money away from commodity bases toward substitute forms. In the early stages of this evolution, the commodity bases of money remained, but *claims* to the commodity increasingly served as the standard monetary unit, more than did the standard commodity itself. The next stage, bringing us to the present, consisted of removing the commodity basis of money, leaving the claims *per se* to fulfill the functions of money—the cat has disappeared, but the smile remains.

The highest evolutionary form of money today is the debt of banks in the form of deposit accounts. Nothing "backs" such money, except other paper claims. When a depositor exercises his claim against a bank by writing a check on his account, the result is merely a transfer of his claim against the bank to someone else. If a depositor exercises his claim by demanding coins or currency from the bank, another kind of paper claim is substituted for the one given up. Although coins have some metal value, the metallic content usually has a lower market value than the coins as money. In the case of paper currency, Federal Reserve Notes are just that—paper—which can be exchanged for other paper claims but not for any specified standard commodity at a fixed ratio.

Notwithstanding the apparently tenuous nature of modern money, people generally accept it in payments, mainly because it has become customary and conventional to do so. (Money's property of being *legal tender*—i.e., a legal means of discharging debts—is also involved, but this is of secondary importance.) You accept what passes for money because you know that other people will accept it in turn.

In short, the value of modern money is no longer related to its commodity backing. Rather, its value is determined by its *purchasing power* over goods and services in general; it varies inversely with changes in the average level of prices, as measured by the movement of price indexes (see Chapter 2).

2 Coins and Currency Circulation

As the volume of small retail and service transactions varies, so accordingly varies the public's need for coins and paper currency. If a greater quantity is required for convenience, the demand first appears at banks, with customers cashing checks in excess of other customer deposits of coins and currency. When banks find their vault holdings of coins and currency falling below normal levels, they purchase additional amounts from Federal Reserve Banks (quasi-public institutions, described in Chapter 9). Federal Reserve Banks in turn purchase additional coins from the U.S. Treasury Department and request permission to issue additional paper currency in the form of Federal Reserve Notes. Thus, if the public demands more coins and currency, unless stocks on hand are sufficient, more is coined and printed to fulfill the demand.

In day-to-day transactions, banks pay out coins and currency to some customers and receive them for deposit from other customers. Only if the outflow and inflow fail to equal each other is there a net increase or decrease of coins and currency in circulation. If the public demand for coins and currency falls (as, for instance, during the several weeks after Christmas), the excess amount is deposited in banks, which may deposit them in turn in Federal Reserve Banks.

Coin and currency circulation does not directly affect total money supply. The public acquires additional coins and currency by drawing upon deposit accounts. Hence, bank deposit money in existence decreases by the same amount as any net increase of coins and currency in circulation. If coin and currency circulation decreases—*i.e.,* more is deposited in banks than withdrawn—bank deposit money increases to the same extent.

3   Bank Deposit Creation

Individual bank deposits may be acquired by (*a*) the deposit of coins or currency, (*b*) the deposit of checks, or (*c*) as the proceeds of a bank loan or financial investment.

For the economy as a whole, coin and currency deposits result in an increase in bank deposit money only if coins and currency in circulation *decrease.* While this tends to occur in certain seasons of each year, over the years coin and currency circulation tends to *increase,* reflecting a growing volume of small retail and service transactions. Instead, then, of coin and currency circulation constituting a source of bank deposit money, in the long run this circulation has a negative influence on bank deposit supply.

The deposit of checks written on commercial banks has no effect on the total amount of bank deposits in the economy. When X deposits to his account a check written by Y, the deposit account of Y decreases to the same extent that X's account increases. (The deposit of a check written against a Federal Reserve Bank is in a different category, as will be seen in the next chapter.)

There remain bank *loans and financial investments,* and these not only contribute to the amount of individual bank deposits, but to the economy's supply of bank deposit money as well. When a bank makes a loan or financial investment, the deposit account of the borrower or seller of the security to the bank is credited (increased) by the amount of the loan or value of the security sold. Since no one else's deposit account is affected by this transaction, the total amount of bank deposits in the economy is increased.

The *repayment* of bank loans and financial disinvestments by banks destroy bank deposits. When a borrower repays a bank loan, his bank account is accordingly reduced. In a similar manner, the purchase of a security from a bank causes the buyer's bank account to decrease by the value of the security. Physically, the disappearance of bank deposits simply consists of bookkeeping entries, just as the creation of bank deposits.

For any given period, changes in the economy's total supply of bank deposits depend upon whether their creation through bank loans and financial investments exceeds or falls short of their destruction through loan repayments and financial disinvestments. Historically, new loans and financial investments have far exceeded repayments and disinvestments, leaving a net accumulation of deposits. Except in recession periods, this tends to be true year-by-year, with the supply of bank deposit money steadily growing with the economy.

D CONFUSIONS TO AVOID

1 Demand Deposits and "Real" Money

People have a strong tendency to think of money as "really" consisting of only coins and currency, with bank deposits being only a kind of surrogate money.

The worst confusion resulting from this misunderstanding is to think of bank deposits as *consisting* of coins and currency. They do not. They have an independent existence, and they consist only of bookkeeping entries.

A related confusion is that banks *lend* their deposits. Since banks do not *own*, but rather *owe*, their deposit liabilities, they clearly cannot lend them. The money banks lend in the form of deposit accounts is *created* by the banks. (There are limitations on the ability of banks to create money, as will be shown in the next chapter.)

2 The Different Meanings of "Deposit"

Much confusion arises out of the three different meanings of the word *deposit*. The term is used to refer to *that which is deposited* in a bank—such as currency or checks. It is also used as a verb—*the act of depositing* something in the bank.

But when we speak of bank deposits as part of the money supply, we have the third meaning in mind: bank deposits as *demand claims* against the bank its liabilities.

3   The Dollar and its Gold "Backing"

Within the United States, the last connection between the dollar and gold
was severed in 1968. (The dollar is still tied to gold for international purposes.)
It is not true therefore to say that the dollar is valuable because of its gold backing. But then this never was a valid statement. The value of the American dollar
is determined by its purchasing power. If the value of the dollar declines (as it
has tended to over the years), the explanation lies mainly in the presence of
excessive aggregate demand causing inflation, as shown in Chapter 5.

CHAPTER 9 MONETARY CONTROLS

A PRINCIPLES

1 Absence of Effective Controls on Coins and Currency

There are no effective limitations on the minting of coins or the issuance of paper currency, even though Federal Reserve Banks are required to maintain 100 percent collateral (in the form of government securities) against their note issues. No useful purpose would be served by setting limits on coin and currency supply, since their circulation does not affect total money supply.

2 Limitations on Bank Deposit Creation

The creation of bank deposit money is limited by the necessity that banks maintain *reserves* against their deposit liabilities.

    a. As a general rule, a single bank in a system of banks cannot create additional deposit money through loans and financial investments in an amount greater than the bank's *excess reserves.*

    b. The banking system as a whole can create new deposit money in an amount that is a multiple of the system's excess reserves, the magnitude of the multiple being determined by the percentage of *required reserves.*

3 Nature and Sources of Bank Reserves

    a. In the United States, member banks of the Federal Reserve System are required to hold *legal reserves* in the form of *deposit accounts* with a

Federal Reserve Bank and/or in the form of *vault cash.* In practice, only a minor fraction of a bank's legal reserves is normally held in vault cash.

(*Nonmember* banks are subject to reserve requirements determined by the state in which the bank is located. Since the banking system in the United States is dominated by *member* banks in the Federal Reserve System, the remainder of the discussion will concern member banks only.)

b. An individual bank *acquires* reserves when it receives coins and currency or checks written on other commercial banks from its customers. A bank *loses* reserves when its customers withdraw coins and currency or write checks which are deposited in other banks.

c. The commercial banking system acquires reserves principally as a result of Federal Reserve Bank *open-market purchases* of securities and *loans.* The system *loses* reserves primarily as a result of the *open-market sale* of securities by Federal Reserve Banks and the repayment of loans from Reserve Banks.

4 Federal Reserve Controls

Federal Reserve Banks control the ability of commercial banks to create deposit money chiefly through controlling the amount and cost of commercial bank reserves. The *amount* of reserves is controlled by *open-market operations.* Excess reserves are additionally controlled through changes in *reserve requirements.* The *cost* of reserves is controlled through the *discount rate* set by Federal Reserve Banks on loans extended to commercial banks.

In summary, the three primary instruments of Federal Reserve control over the supply of bank deposit money are: *open-market operations,* changes in *reserve requirements,* and changes in the *discount rate.*

To *expand* the money-creating ability of commercial banks, Federal Reserve Banks may engage in open-market purchases, or lower reserve requirements, or lower the discount rate.

To *contract,* or retard, the growth of money supply, Reserve Banks may engage in open-market sales, or raise reserve requirements, or increase the discount rate.

B CONCEPTS

1 The Federal Reserve System

The Federal Reserve System is the *central banking system* of the United

States. A central bank, differing from private banks, operates as a *public service* institution, with the principal objective of exercising controls over the monetary affairs of the country as a whole.

The System consists of 12 regional Federal Reserve Banks, each under the supervision of a Board of Directors. Even though Reserve Banks are owned privately by member banks, overall direction in important policy matters is vested in a seven-man Board of Governors, appointed by the President with the advice and consent of the Senate. The Board of Governors is responsible for the *monetary policy* of the country.

2 Bank Reserves

a. The *legal reserves* of a bank are those which are acceptable in meeting the reserve requirements set by the monetary authority.

b. The *excess reserves* of a bank are the legal reserves which it holds beyond the amount it is required to hold.

c. *Required reserves* are those which a bank must hold to conform to the requirements of Federal Reserve Banks (or state authorities in the case of nonmember banks).

Reserve requirements are stated in terms of a minimum *percentage* of a bank's *deposit liabilities.* For example, if reserve requirements are 16 percent, a bank is obliged to hold reserves equal at least to 16 percent of its outstanding deposit liabilities.

d. Bank deposits in Federal Banks, which constitute the primary form of legal reserves, are *assets* to the banks owning the deposits and *liabilities* of the Federal Reserve Bank in which they are held. Like customer deposits in a commercial bank, commercial bank deposits in a Federal Reserve Bank consist simply of bookkeeping entries.

e. Reserves in the form of *vault cash* consist of coins and paper currency which a bank has in its possession.

3 Member and Nonmember Banks

A *member* bank is a bank belonging to the Federal Reserve System. All banks with charters from the federal government (*national* banks) are *required* to be member banks. Banks with charters from their state governments may or may not belong to the Federal Reserve System. Those choosing not to join are *nonmember* banks.

4 Open-Market Operations

The most commonly used and important instrument of Federal Reserve control is *open-market operations*. These consist of Federal Reserve Bank purchases or sales of securities (in practice, government securities) in the market. The "market" is composed of banks, insurance companies, building and loan associations, manufacturing firms, individuals, and any other organizations interested in buying or selling securities.

5 The Discount Rate

The *discount rate* is the rate of interest charged by Federal Reserve Banks on advances or loans extended to member banks.

C DISCUSSION

1 The Absence of Coin and Currency Controls

Coins and paper currency are made available to the public for convenience in transacting small retail and service trade. Failure to satisfy public demand would only result in the inconveniences associated with a shortage—the difficulties of making "change." Since coins and currency are acquired by the public through drawing upon bank deposit accounts, the total supply of money is not affected by the amount in circulation. Thus, there is no rational basis for limiting the amount of coins and paper currency which may be issued by the Treasury and Federal Reserve Banks. Legal requirements prescribing the metallic content of coins and 100 percent collateral as government securities against Federal Reserve notes are merely formal vestiges of an earlier day without current relevance. (However, when coins are minted whose metal content exceeds the nominal value of the coins, they are melted down and sold, with a resulting shortage of coins for monetary use.)

2 The Need for Reserves

Even without legal requirements, a bank would have to maintain reserves against its deposit liabilities. Reserves are necessary to meet claims against the bank arising out of a *net* withdrawal of coins and currency by customers and *adverse clearing balances* with other banks in the system.

Vault cash reserves are kept to serve the first type of claim, but only a small fraction of deposit liabilities is needed for this purpose. While a bank is constantly being asked for coins and currency, it is at the same time constantly receiving them. Provision has to be made only for any excess of withdrawals over receipts that might occur occasionally.

Much more important are the claims against a bank arising out of adverse clearing balances. An *adverse clearing balance* develops when, over any given period, a greater total amount of checks against accounts held in the bank is deposited in other banks than the total amount of checks written against other banks received for deposit. In such a case, the bank is confronted with a net claim against it by other banks which it must be prepared to pay off. The normal way of discharging the claim is by drawing upon the *deposit account* held with a *Federal Reserve Bank—i.e.,* by drawing upon the bank's *reserve* account.

Of course, a bank does not expect constantly to have an adverse clearing balance; normally, favorable clearing balances occur with about the same frequency. *Favorable clearing balances* give a bank net claims against other banks and provide reserves. Thus, as with currency circulation, a bank needs to maintain only enough reserve deposits to meet any probable excess of adverse over favorable clearing balances. Discretion in this decision, however, is largely removed by reserve requirements set by the monetary authority.

3 Reserves and Money Creation by a Single Bank

When a bank receives coins and currency or checks written on other banks for deposit to a customer's account, the deposit liabilities of the bank increase, but so too do its reserves. Deposited coins and currency are added to the bank's *vault cash* reserves, the checks add to its *clearing* claims which, when settled, increase its *reserve account* with a Federal Reserve Bank.

In contrast, when a bank creates a new deposit by making a loan or financial investment, there is no matching acquisition of reserves. On the contrary, the bank can expect to *lose reserves* as a result of the operation, and, in fact, to play it safely, *the bank must expect to lose as much reserves as the amount of the loan or investment.*

To see why this is so, consider what happens when a bank makes a loan of, say, $100 thousand. The borrower receives the loan in the form of an addition to his deposit account in the bank. But the new deposit is not likely to remain in the bank: it is not usual for money to be borrowed and the interest costs of the loan incurred unless it is meant to be spent. The money is spent, typically by writing checks. Recipients of these checks deposit them in their bank accounts. With thousands of banks in the system, the probability is that such accounts will be in banks other than the borrower's. As a consequence, the lending bank finds that its *clearing balance* with other banks will be adversely affected by roughly the amount of the loan or investment it made. The bank's reserves are thus drawn down in settlement of its clearing debt.

The conclusion emerging from this analysis is that a bank cannot prudently create new deposit money through loans and investments in an amount greater than its *excess reserves*. The maximum amount of reserves a bank can lose without falling short of minimum reserve requirements is its excess reserves. If a $100 thousand loan leads to the loss of $100 thousand of reserves, before granting the loan the bank should have excess reserves in this amount.

In summary, a *single* bank's money-creating powers is limited by the amount of the excess reserves which it possesses.

4 Multiple Bank Credit Expansion in the System

What is true for a single bank is *not* true for the banking system, *i.e.,* all banks taken together. While a single bank loses reserves as the result of creating new deposit money, the *system* cannot lose reserves: reserves lost by one bank are gained by other banks. Consequently, while a single bank is limited in its deposit-creating ability by the amount of its excess reserves, the limits on the banking system are much broader. With excess reserves of $100 thousand, the banking system can expand deposits by a multiple of that amount which equals the *reciprocal of the reserve requirement*. If the reserve requirement is 20 percent, the multiple is 5 (100/20); if the requirement is 10 percent, the multiple is 10 (100/10), etc.

How multiple credit expansion works can best be seen through a simplified example. Let us begin with Bank A having in its possession $100 of excess reserves. Bank A now makes loans and investments of $100, thereby creating $100 of new deposit liabilities. We assume that the whole amount of these deposits is spent, and that the checks are placed on deposit by their recipients in Bank B.

Bank B has thus acquired $100 of new deposits and, upon collecting its clearing claim against Bank A, an extra $100 of reserves. Assuming a reserve requirement of 20 percent, Bank B's excess reserves have increased $80, equal to the $100 of new reserves, minus the $20 of required reserves against its additional deposit liabilities. Bank B is therefore in a safe position to lend or financially invest an amount equal to its excess reserves of $80; if it proceeds to do so, it creates additional deposit money in the same amount. Again assume that the newly created deposits in B are spent and end up in the accounts of customers of Bank C.

Bank C thus acquires new deposits of $80 and collects $80 of reserves from Bank B. Bank C is required to hold only $16 of reserves against its new deposit liabilities (20 percent of $80), leaving it with excess reserves of $64. Bank C in turn makes loans and investments equal to its excess reserves of $64, with the subsequent pattern the same as previously.

The result is the creation of new deposit money totaling the sum of

$100 + $80 + $64 + ... This is equivalent to $100 + 100 (8/10) + 100 (8/10)^2 + ...$, a geometric series the sum of which is $100 \times 1/(1-8/10) = 500. It should be noted that the same result is obtained by multiplying the excess reserves of $100 by the reciprocal of the reserve requirement of 20 percent, or 5. To observe the result in still another way, $100 in reserves support $500 in demand deposits if the reserve requirement is 20 percent—for $100 is 20 percent of $500.

5 Sources of Reserves for the System

Federal Reserve loans and open-market purchases increase bank reserves in the following manner: when a member bank borrows from a Reserve Bank, the proceeds of the loan are added to the commercial bank's deposit account with the Reserve Bank; this is the main component of the bank's legal reserves. When the Fed makes open-market purchases, it pays for the securities by writing a check against itself. If a commercial bank is the seller of the security, it deposits the check in its account with a Reserve Bank. If the seller of the security is not a bank, the check is deposited by the seller in his bank, which in turn deposits it in a Reserve Bank. In either case, the reserve account of member banks is increased.

Open-market sales by the Fed have opposite effects. The checks written by purchasers lead to a reduction in member bank reserve deposits. The repayment by banks of loans from Reserve Banks also cause a reduction in bank reserves, since the payoff is made by drawing upon the banks' reserve accounts.

6 Federal Reserve Controls

The ability of banks to create deposit money depends upon their reserve position; by determining the amount of reserves through its loan and open-market policies, the Federal Reserve authorities can set *upper limits* on the economy's supply of money. If the Federal Reserve wishes to slow down or stop the creation of additional money supply, the system's reserves can be reduced through open-market sales.

Alternatively, or as supplementary measures, an increase in reserve requirements or raising the discount rate can be employed as restrictive devices. While an increase in reserve requirements (within the limits prescribed by Congress) does not affect the quantity of reserves, it reduces *excess* reserves upon which the ability of banks to create new money depends. Raising the discount rate also does not directly affect reserves, but by making it more costly for banks to acquire reserves through borrowing from Reserve Banks, it tends to *discourage* banks from acquiring reserves.

While the Federal Reserve authorities can always *restrict* money supply through these measures, their power to *expand* money supply is much more limited. Increasing reserves through open-market purchases, enlarging excess reserves through reducing reserve requirements, and making it cheaper for banks to borrow reserves by lowering the discount rate, make it possible and easier for banks to expand their loans and investments, they do not in fact assure that they will do so. Bank loans depend upon customer demand: even if loans are offered at attractive interest rates, the response may be weak if business conditions are not promising. While banks may take the initiative themselves and make financial investments, these too may not be sufficiently attractive to induce a significant expansion in volume.

The implications of this asymmetry in the influence of Federal Reserve policies on money supply will be discussed in the next chapter.

D CONFUSIONS TO AVOID

1 Legal and Excess Reserves

Legal reserves are reserves in the forms required by law; excess reserves consist of legal reserves not currently being used to meet reserve requirements. While all excess reserves are legal reserves, not all legal reserves are excess reserves.

2 The Single Bank versus the System of Banks

Keep in mind that while an individual bank ordinarily cannot create new deposit money greater than its excess reserves, all banks taken together can create new money by a *multiple* of excess reserves.

3 Reserves and Money Creation

Banks cannot make new loans and investments and create additional money without possessing excess reserves. But this does not mean that banks lend and invest their reserves. The money banks lend and invest is *created* by them; reserves are necessary to permit banks to engage in the money-creating process.

CHAPTER 10 MONETARY POLICY

A PRINCIPLES

1 Money Supply and the National Income

a. The supply of money influences the national income to the extent that it affects *expenditure on goods and services.*

b. Other things being equal, the larger the quantity of money in circulation the greater the aggregate spending and national income tend to be. The influence of money supply on spending is transmitted primarily through the *rate of interest.*

2 Demand for and Supply of Money

a. The *demand* for money is based on *transaction* and *precautionary* purposes. At a given level of national income, the quantity of money demanded is inversely related to the rate of interest. A change in national income causes the whole demand schedule for money to shift in the same direction as the change in national income.

b. The *supply* of money is determined by Federal Reserve policy.

3 The Rate of Interest

The *rate of interest* is determined by the interaction of the demand for and the supply of money. An increase in the demand for money, the supply remaining constant, causes the interest rate to rise. A similar effect is produced by a decreased supply of money if the demand remains constant.

The interest rate falls in response to an increased supply or decreased demand for money.

4 Countercyclical Monetary Policy

a. To promote recovery from a *recession* or to prevent one, an "easy" money policy—consisting of enlarging banks' excess reserves and lowering the interest rate—is instituted.

b. To prevent or combat *inflation,* a "tight" money policy—reducing excess reserves and raising the interest rate—is called for.

5 Monetary Policy versus Fiscal Policy

Monetary policy may be used in lieu of or in combination with *fiscal* policy. The advantages of monetary policy over fiscal policy include its quicker applicability and its noninterference with the role of government in the allocation of resources. The disadvantages of monetary policy are its possible lack of effectiveness—especially in periods of recession—and the threat it may pose to economic growth during periods of "tight" money.

B CONCEPTS

1 The Supply of Money

By *supply of money,* the quantity of coins, paper currency, and bank deposits in the possession of the nonbank public is meant.

2 The Demand for Money

The *demand for money* is a *schedule* showing the quantity of money the public wishes to possess at various rates of interest. An increase or decrease in demand is indicated by an increase or decrease in the quantity demanded at *each* rate of interest.

In diagrammatic form the demand for money appears as a curve of the general shape shown in Figure 10.1 by DD or $D'D'$.

Movement along DD (or $D'D'$) indicates a change in the quantity of money (M) demanded as a result of a change in the rate of interest (i). Movement from

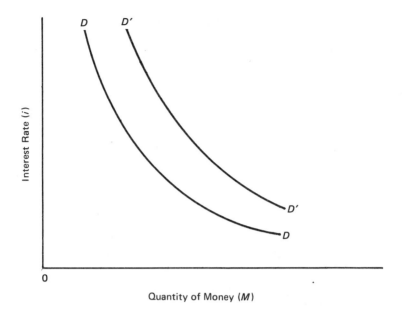

FIGURE 10.1   The Demand Curve for Money

one curve to the other indicates a *shift* in demand, occurring independently of a change in the interest rate. A shift from *DD* to *D'D'* represents an *increase* in demand; from *D'D'* to *DD*, a *decrease* in demand.

3   Transactions and Precautionary Demand

The *transactions* motive for holding money arises out of the need to main-tain a certain amount of money to conduct ordinary business affairs. For each active participant in the economy, there is a flow of money receipts and expendi-tures. Rarely over short periods do the inflow and outflow match each other either in amount or in timing. During the interval between receipts and pay-ments, money balances are held.

Normally, more money is held by the public than the minimum amount necessary for convenience in carrying on current transactions. The extra money is held for *precautionary* motives. The role of money in this connection is that of a 100 percent *liquid asset—i.e.,* an asset which can be used at face value for spending at any time.

Holding some portion of assets in liquid form allows meeting unanticipated expenditures or delays in money receipts and taking advantage of profitable in-vestment opportunities that may come along.

4   The Rate of Interest

The *rate* of interest is the *price* of credit or borrowed money per year. It is expressed as a percentage of the principal amount: if, for example, it costs $5 per year to borrow $100, the rate of interest is 5/100 or 5 percent.

Different rates of interest reflect different kinds of loans: rates on *short-term* loans usually differ from those on *long-term* ones. Loans of higher *risk* carry greater rates than those with smaller risk. The basic, or "pure," rate of interest is that applying to riskless loans.

5   "Easy" and "Tight" Money

Money is said to be "easy" when credit or loanable funds are readily available to borrowers, and the interest rate is low. An easy monetary policy is one producing easy money conditions.

"Tight" money exists when credit or loans are difficult to obtain, and the interest rate is high. A tight monetary policy is one which causes tight money conditions.

C   DISCUSSION

1   Money and the National Income

The national income is equal to the aggregate annual expenditure on currently produced goods and services (see Chapter 2). Aggregate expenditure may be expressed as the product of the amount of money in circulation (M) and the average number of times each dollar of the money supply is spent. The latter is called the *velocity of circulation* of money, represented by V. If V is defined to include expenditure only on currently produced goods and services (the *income-velocity* of circulation), the following, known as the *equation of exchange,* results:

$$MV = Y$$

(NOTE: Y stands for national income; in some formulations, Y is replaced by its equivalent PT, where P represents the average level of prices of goods and services and T is the physical volume of production of goods and services.)

The equation of exchange shows a possible close relation between the supply of money and the national income. But it does *not* necessarily indicate a one-to-one relationship, which would hold only if the velocity of circulation remains constant. If M should increase, accompanied by a proportional decrease in V, the aggregate expenditure and the national income, M multiplied by V, would remain unaffected. This emphasizes the important point that money supply affects the national income only to the extent that it affects aggregate *spending*. Money that is not spent has no direct influence on income.

2   The Rate of Interest and Aggregate Expenditure

Among the variables influencing aggregate spending on goods and services, the rate of interest is considered important because all the components of expenditure are susceptible to its influence. For example, consumption expenditure, even though primarily determined by disposable personal income, is at least marginally affected by the interest rate: high interest rates probably encourage greater saving and increase the cost of consumer credit. Government spending, especially at the state and local level, is affected by interest rates since the cost of projects such as school and road construction financed with borrowed funds varies with the rate of interest.

The closest relationship between the interest rate and spending holds with respect to *investment* expenditure. In determining whether a given investment expenditure should be made, a business firm compares the *expected rate of return* on the investment (called the *marginal efficiency of investment*) with the prevailing rate of interest. After taking risk factors into account, firms tend to carry investments up to the point at which the marginal efficiency of investment is *equal* to the rate of interest. For example, suppose that a firm can borrow money capital at a 5 percent rate of interest, and that an investment project costs $100 thousand to construct. Assume that each year the investment is expected to yield an *extra revenue* to the firm—after deducting all *extra costs* except for interest costs—of $10 thousand. The expected net rate of return, or marginal efficiency, of the investment is therefore 10 percent per year. Since the necessary money capital can be borrowed at an interest cost of only $5 thousand a year, it would obviously pay the firm to make the investment (unless the risk factor is considered too great). Profit opportunities are not exhausted until (again, apart from the risk factor) the marginal efficiency of capital is *equal* to the interest rate.

For the economy as a whole, the marginal efficiency of capital *decreases* the greater the volume of investment, assuming that the state of technology and other things remain constant. This is shown in Figure 10.2 by the right-to-left slope of the marginal efficiency investment curve *II*. The marginal efficiency of investment declines as the quantity of investment increases because the best investment opportunities are seized first. (The more fundamental reason is the Law of Diminishing Returns, described in Chapter 15.) With the marginal efficiency of capital and the interest rate (r) measured vertically and the volume of investment (*i*) measured horizontally, Figure 10.2 shows that at interest rate *Or*, investment expenditure would tend to be *Oi*; with a lower interest rate *Or'*, investment would be *Oi'*.

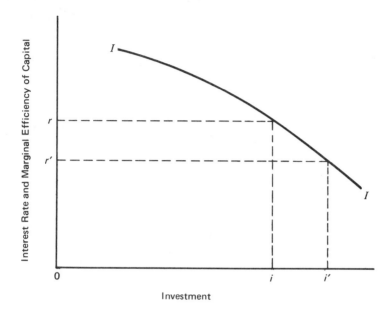

FIGURE 10.2 The Marginal Efficiency of Investment

3 The Demand and Supply of Money and the Rate of Interest

Given the national income, the quantity of money demanded by the public is greater at a lower rate of interest than at a higher rate. Why? Because, although there are advantages in holding assets in the 100 percent liquid form of money, sacrificing *interest income* becomes a *cost*. If the market rate of interest on safe loans is 5 percent, each $100 of money withheld sacrifices income at the rate of $5 per year. Thus, when the interest rate is high, the public will wish to minimize their money balances; when the interest rate is low, larger money balances are desired.

While the *precautionary* demand for money is primarily related to the interest rate, the *transactions* demand depends on the level of the *national income.* The greater the national income, the more money needed to carry on transactions conveniently. A change in national income, therefore, causes a *shift* in the position of the demand curve for money.

Given the public demand for money, and the supply of money as determined by the monetary authorities, the market rate of interest tends to settle at the level at which the quantity of money demanded is equal to the quantity supplied. This is shown in Figure 10.3. With the quantity of money measured horizontally and the rate of interest measured vertically, DD is the demand curve for money. If the supply curve of money is SS, the rate of interest tends to be Or. A greater supply of money, $S'S'$, leads to a lower rate of interest, Or'.

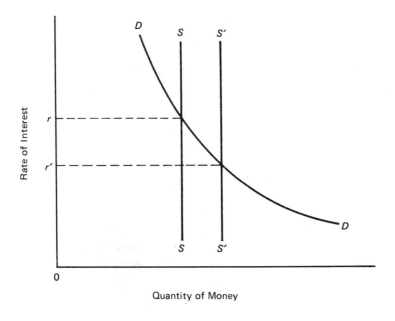

FIGURE 10.3 Demand and Supply of Money and the Rate of Interest

4 Countercyclical Monetary Policy

An increase in money supply will tend to expand or prevent the contraction of aggregate expenditure and national income. Lowering the interest rate (or preventing it from rising) would encourage greater expenditure, especially investment. To retard increases in aggregate expenditure, a slowdown in the growth of money supply, thereby raising the interest rate, would be necessary.

Monetary policy is more likely to be effective in controlling the national income in periods of prosperity or inflation. In recession periods, an easy money policy may fail to bring a response of increased expenditure because of the importance of nonmonetary influences, such as a pessimistic outlook, the absence of promising investment opportunities, etc. A lower limit to which the interest rate can be effectively pushed contributes to this conclusion. (A lower limit on the interest rate occurs because at some point the low cost of holding money induces the public to absorb additional money supply in idle balances. Thus, an excess supply of money, which otherwise would force the interest rate downward, is prevented from developing.)

On the other hand, a tight monetary policy can push up the interest rate to the level required to contract expenditure.

In periods of inflation, one serious disadvantage of monetary compared to fiscal policy is the possibility of its retarding economic growth. This may occur because of the primary impact of the interest rate on *investment,* which provides increased productive capacity for the future. The construction industry especially tends to bear the brunt of higher interest rates.

D   CONFUSIONS TO AVOID

1   Money and Income

Money is not to be confused with income. Income is received in the form of money, but as a flow of money over time. The supply of money refers to the *stock* of money on hand at a particular point in time. Money stock is converted into a flow when it is multiplied by the velocity of circulation. Thus, aggregate expenditure or national income of, say, $750 billion is supported by a money stock of $150 billion if the income-velocity of circulation of money averages 5.

2   The Demand for Money

The demand for money should be thought of as the quantity of money the public wishes to possess, allowing for the *cost* of holding it (the interest rate) and the available alternative forms of holding assets. Instead of holding money, stocks, bonds, real estate, and numerous other kinds of assets can be purchased. The advantage of holding money derives from its property of complete *liquidity.* The advantage of the other asset forms is that they usually yield an *income return* or have the prospect of increasing in value (capital appreciation). Asset holdings are therefore divided between money and other forms; the interest rate usually determines the proportion.

CHAPTER 11 INTERNATIONAL MONETARY RELATIONS

A PRINCIPLES

1 Domestic versus International Money

The special problems of international monetary relations arise from the existence of separate national monetary units and fiscal and monetary policies. (For short, the phrase "national currency" is used to refer to "national monetary unit.")

2 Foreign Exchange Rates

National currencies are related to each other through exchange rates, permitting international price comparisons. A *foreign exchange rate* is the price of one national currency expressed in terms of another.

3 The Balance of Payments and the Demand and Supply of Foreign Exchange

The balance of payments of a country is a summary statement of its *international payments and receipts* over a given period of time. The *payments* entries in the balance of payments give rise to a *demand* for foreign exchange; the *receipts* entries account for a *supply* of foreign exchange.

4   Balance of Payments Equilibrium and Disequilibrium

The balance of payments is in *equilibrium* when the total ordinary international payments of a country equals its total ordinary international receipts. If payments exceed receipts, the balance of payments is in a *deficit* disequilibrium; if receipts exceed payments, there is a balance of payments *surplus* disequilibrium.

5   The Rate of Exchange and the Balance of Payments

Other things being equal, the *higher* the rate of exchange, the *greater* a country's international *receipts* and the smaller its international *payments.* At a *lower* rate of exchange, a country's international receipts tend to be *smaller* and its international payments tend to be *larger.* The rate of exchange which equalizes a country's international payments and receipts is the *equilibrium rate of exchange.*

6   Correction of Balance of Payments Disequilibrium

Balance of payments disequilibrium cannot persist indefinitely. A country with a balance of payments *deficit* is compelled sooner or later to eliminate the deficit—*i.e.,* to "correct" (or "adjust") its balance of payments.

The principal processes or methods of correcting a balance of payments deficit include:

allowing or forcing the exchange rate on foreign currencies to *rise*—called currency *devaluation* or *depreciation,*
deflating domestic prices and/or income through "tight" monetary policies or restrictive fiscal policies, and
imposing *direct controls* over international payments.

B   CONCEPTS

1   Foreign Exchange Rates

Foreign exchange is the general term applied to the various instruments or means of making international payments. The rate of exchange is the *price,* in a particular country, of one unit of a foreign currency. For example, in mid-1971 the rate of exchange in the United States on the British pound was approximately $2.40 and on the French franc $0.18.

2 The Balance of Payments

The balance of payments is divided into two columns: "receipts" (or credits) and "payments" (or debits). For each type of transaction, an entry is made in the appropriate column.

Transactions are classified into three major types, or "accounts": *Current Account,* embracing current trade in goods and services; *Capital Account,* which includes all transactions in paper claims and evidences of debt or ownership (international loans and investments, gifts, and grants); and *Official Settlements Account,* which includes all transactions undertaken by official agencies for the purpose of filling the gap between payments and receipts on other transactions, with gold and official capital movements usually the main transactions involved.

Within each of the major accounts, the main payments and receipts entries are as follows:

Balance of Payments Account	Payments	Receipts
Current Account		
Imports of goods and services	X	
Exports of goods and services		X
Capital Account		
Loans and grants to foreign countries	X	
Loans and grants from foreign countries		X
Investments in foreign countries	X	
Foreign investments in home country		X
Official Settlements Account		
Import of gold	X	
Export of gold		X
Increase in official balances held abroad	X	
Increase in foreign official balances held in home country		X

3 The Demand and Supply of Foreign Exchange

The *demand* for foreign exchange is a schedule showing the total quantities of foreign exchange that would be purchased at various rates of exchange. The *supply* of foreign exchange is a similar schedule indicating the quantities of foreign exchange offered for sale at various rates of exchange.

When plotted in a conventional manner, with the rate of exchange (R)

measured vertically and the quantity of foreign exchange (Q) measured horizontally, the demand for foreign exchange appears as a curve falling from left to right, and the supply as a curve normally rising from left to right, as shown in Figure 11.1.

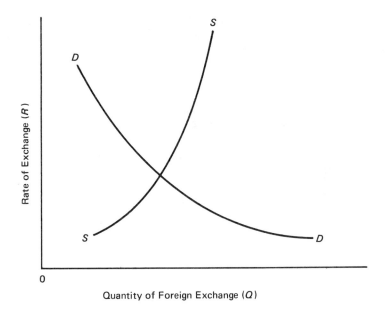

FIGURE 11.1 Demand and Supply Curves of Foreign Exchange

4   Balance of Payments Equilibrium and Disequilibrium

Balance of payments equilibrium is a self-sustaining condition; internal forces do not cause changes in the country's international transactions. This condition prevails if a country's international *receipts* from current-account and capital-account transactions equal in their totality the international *payments* from current and capital-account transactions.

Balance of payments *disequilibrium* is not a self-sustaining situation: it cannot continue indefinitely. Characterized by an *imbalance* between total receipts and total payments in the current and capital accounts, the situation must be matched by an opposite imbalance in the Official Settlements Account. For example, if total receipts on current and capital transactions is $100 million *less* than total payments in these accounts, then the Official Settlements Account receipts must *exceed* payments by $100 million. If a country spends more abroad than its international receipts, the difference must be financed in some manner. The means of financing the difference are recorded in the Official Settlements Account.

Balance of payments disequilibrium manifests itself in a net balance in the Official Settlements Account. If the net balance in this account is *positive* (receipts exceeding payments), a balance of payments *deficit* is shown. For the United States, the positive net official settlements balance usually indicates a *gold outflow,* or the accumulation of foreign-owned dollar balances. If the net balance in the Official Settlements Account is *negative,* this expresses a balance of payments *surplus,* typically showing up for the United States as a *gold inflow* or reduction in foreign-owned dollar balances.

5   Currency Devaluation or Depreciation

The devaluation, or depreciation, of a currency is manifested in a *higher rate of exchange* on other currencies—that is, in a lower international value of the currency. Strictly speaking, *devaluation* occurs when the currency is officially related to gold or some other standard commodity and the gold or standard content of the currency is *reduced*; this results in a rise in exchange rates on other currencies whose gold or standard content remains the same. *Exchange depreciation* describes a rise in exchange rates of those currencies which have no specified official relationship to gold or other standard commodity.

C   DISCUSSION

1   The Balance of Payments and the Foreign Exchange Market

Although there are certain transactions in the balance of payments which do not affect either the demand or the supply of foreign exchange, broadly speaking we may regard payments entries (debits) as equivalent to the *demand* for foreign exchange, and receipts entries (credits) as equivalent to the *supply* of foreign exchange.

2   Balance of Payments Disequilibrium

An imbalance between a country's international payments and receipts on current and capital accounts indicates the presence of disequilibrium; it is a situation containing the seeds of its own modification. This is seen most clearly in the case of a *deficit* disequilibrium (payments > receipts), though it also holds for a *surplus* disequilibrium (receipts > payments).

When there is a deficit in the balance of payments of a country, the excess international payments require some means of financing. As in the case of an individual who spends more than his income, the difference must somehow be made up. A deficit is usually financed by drawing upon a country's international monetary *reserves* in the form of *gold* or accumulated balances of *foreign exchange.* Another method of financing a deficit is international *borrowing.* (One form of borrowing, extensively used by the United States in recent years, is the accumulation of the country's currency by other countries.)

The reason a deficit balance of payments cannot indefinitely persist should now be clear: the means of financing a deficit are limited. A country's supply of gold and foreign exchange reserves and its ability to obtain special international credits and loans sooner or later become exhausted when they have been used to finance a deficit.

3   The Rate of Exchange and the Balance of Payments

The balance of payments of a country is affected by a wide spectrum of domestic and international forces. One of the key variables is the *rate of exchange,* the connecting link between prices in the home country and the rest of the world.

At higher rates of exchange, a country's export goods and services are *cheaper* to the rest of the world than they would be at lower rates of exchange. At an exchange rate of $0.20 per French franc, an American product with a price of $1.00 costs the French 5 francs. At an exchange rate of $0.25 per franc, the cost of the product would be only 4 francs. Ordinarily, foreigners will purchase more the cheaper the exported goods are. Thus, the higher the exchange rate, the greater tends to be the volume of exports and the quantity of foreign exchange earned from exports. (This does not hold if the foreign demand is inelastic, a possibility not presently discussed.)

The quantity of foreign exchange supplied through exports is greater at higher rates of exchange, but the quantity of foreign exchange demanded to pay for imports is *smaller.* As the exchange rates rises, foreign goods *increase* in price to the home country. A French bottle of perfume with a price tag of 100 francs costs an American $20 if the rate of exchange is $0.20 per franc, but $25 if the rate is $0.25 per franc. Since a smaller quantity of imports will be demanded the more expensive they are, the quantity of foreign exchange demanded is *inversely* related to the rate of exchange.

It follows, given the other forces bearing on the balance of payments, that there is a certain *equilibrium rate of exchange* at which a country's balance of payments will be in equilibrium. At any lower rate of exchange, there would be a *deficit* balance of payments; at higher rates a *surplus* balance of payments.

4 Correction of Balance of Payments Disequilibrium

A balance of payments deficit can usually be eliminated by exchange *devaluation,* or *depreciation.* (A surplus disequilibrium would call for currency *appreciation,* or a lowering of exchange rates.)

If, however, a country is committed to a *stable exchange rate* system (as under the gold standard), other ways of correcting balance of payments disequilibrium have to be used. The "classical" method with fixed exchange rates is *internal deflation.*

Instead of raising the exchange rate to reduce the price of a country's exports and make imports more expensive, the same result is accomplished by *lowering the domestic price level.* Alternatively, the national income can be reduced, causing a contraction in the demand for imports as well as for home goods.

In practice, it is nearly impossible today for most countries to deflate—in an absolute sense—the average level of prices. Prices cannot be reduced below costs of production for long; costs are "stuck" almost inflexibly in a downward direction because of labor union resistance to wage decreases and the pricing policies of oligopolistic industries. (On this point, see Chapter 16.)

An attempt to deflate prices is very likely to result in a contraction of production and national income. This, though effective in reducing a balance of payments deficit, is stronger medicine than most countries are willing to take.

Because the classical method of correcting a balance of payments deficit with fixed exchange rates is not popular, recourse to another, very "unclassical," device is common. To eliminate an excess demand for foreign exchange, the government may forcibly contract the market demand by requiring a license to purchase foreign exchange. Or, more mildly, taxes (tariffs) on imported goods may be raised, making imports more expensive to domestic buyers. These are impositions of *direct controls.* There are strong objections to such controls because they interfere with the optimum volume and pattern of international trade and investment. But if there are no acceptable alternative means of correcting a balance of payments deficit, controls can be expected to be used.

D CONFUSIONS TO AVOID

1 Foreign Exchange Rates

Rates of exchange between two currencies are *reciprocals* of each other in the two countries. If the rate in New York is $0.20 on the French franc, the rate in Paris on the dollar is 5 francs (20/100 is the reciprocal of 5). When a change in rates is talked about, it is essential to be clear about the reference point. A *rise* in the dollar rate on the franc is equivalent to a *fall* in the franc rate on the dollar, and vice-versa.

2 The Balance of Payments

The word *balance* in balance of payments does *not* mean, as it may suggest, a net difference between payments and receipts. A balance of payments is a statement, in summary form, of *all* international economic and monetary transactions.

3 "Balance" and "Equilibrium" in the Balance of Payments

The total of a country's entire international payments and all its international receipts as recorded in its balance of payments for any given period of time *must be equal.* This is because of the *double-entry* system employed, in which every payment is matched by a receipt of equal amount, and vice versa.

A *deficit* (excess payments) or *surplus* (excess receipts) in the balance of payments therefore obviously cannot refer to *total* payments and receipts. Instead, they refer to payments and receipts on the combined Current and Capital Accounts, *excluding* the Official Settlements Account. Any imbalance in the former accounts is matched by an opposite imbalance in the latter account, making the grand totals of payments and receipts equal. Thus, equilibrium in the balance of payments (balance of payments and receipts in the first two accounts combined) is quite different from the overall total balance of payments and receipts in *all* accounts.

CHAPTER **12** SUPPLY, DEMAND,
AND PRICE

A PRINCIPLES

1 The Law of Supply and Demand

In a purely competitive market, the price of a good tends to settle at that level at which the *quantity demanded* equals the *quantity supplied*—the *equilibrium price.*

2 Changes in Supply and Demand

An increase in demand or decrease in supply normally causes the price of a good to *rise.* A decrease in demand or increase in supply normally causes the price of a good to *fall.*

3 Price-Elasticity of Supply and Demand and Price and Quantity Changes

The less elastic are demand and supply, the greater the price changes and the smaller the quantity changes caused by a change in demand or supply.

At one limit, a change in demand causes only the price to change, without change in quantity purchased, if supply is *zero elastic* (or *infinitely inelastic*). At the other limit, a change in demand causes only the quantity to change, without change in price, if the supply is *infinitely elastic.*

Correspondingly, shifts in supply affect only price if demand is zero elastic, and affect only quantity if demand is infinitely elastic.

B CONCEPTS

1 Supply and Demand and Quantities Demanded and Supplied

Supply and demand are each *schedules* showing the relationships among various hypothetical prices of a good and the corresponding quantities of the good that would be purchased (demanded) or offered for sale (supplied) at each price.

The demand schedule should be read as, "If such-and-such price were to prevail, then so-and-so quantity of the good would be demanded." The supply schedule should be read as, "If such-and-such price were to prevail, then so-and-so quantity of the good would be supplied."

Supply and demand schedules may be presented in tabular or graph form. In the table that follows, the first and second columns constitute a partial demand schedule, while the first and third columns constitute a partial supply schedule.

Price Per Unit	Quantity Demanded (in physical units)	Quantity Supplied (in physical units)
$1.00	500	900
.95	550	850
.90	600	800
.85	650	750
.80	700	700
.75	750	650

If these hypothetical data are put in diagram form, with price (P) measured vertically and quantity (Q) horizontally, the step-like "curves" of Figure 12.1 are obtained. If it is assumed that between the intervals given in the schedules the same price-quantity relationships hold as for those specified, the curves may be smoothed out as drawn.

It is essential to differentiate clearly between demand or supply and quantity demanded or supplied. Demand refers to the *schedule* or *curve* in its *entirety*, as does supply. The *quantity demanded* or *quantity supplied* refers to a *particular* price and associated quantity. Thus, referring to the above schedule, at a price of $0.90, 600 units are demanded and 800 units are supplied. These quantities demanded and supplied appear as points on demand and supply curves, respectively. While a change in supply or demand involves a shift in the supply or demand curve, a change in quantity demanded or supplied involves only a movement along a given demand or supply curve. An *increase* in demand is reflected by a movement of the demand curve upward and to the right; a *decrease* in demand by a movement of the curve downward and to the left. An *increase* in supply is represented by a movement of the supply curve downward and to the right; a decrease in supply, by a movement upward and to the left.

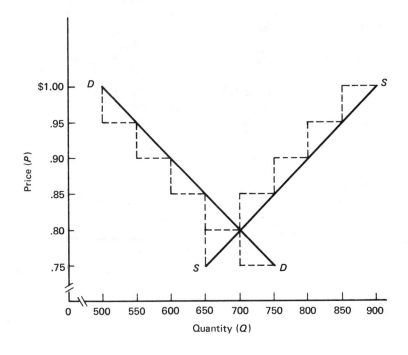

FIGURE 12.1 Supply and Demand Curves

2 Price-Elasticity of Supply and Demand

a. The price-elasticity of supply and demand is a measure of the degree of *responsiveness* of the quantity demanded or supplied to a *change in the unit price* of a good. The assumption is that price is the *independent* variable, quantity the *dependent* variable—that is, quantity changes occur as a result of a prior change in price, unless the whole schedule or curve shifts position.

b. The *coefficient of elasticity* is a numerical measure of the degree of elasticity. It is found by dividing the percentage change in the quantity demanded or supplied by the percentage change in unit price. Letting E_d represent elasticity of demand, E_s elasticity of supply, P unit price, Q_d quantity demanded, Q_s quantity supplied, and the symbol Δ change:

$$E_d = \frac{\dfrac{\Delta Q_d}{Q_d}}{\dfrac{\Delta P}{P}}$$

$$E_s = \frac{\dfrac{\Delta Q_s}{Q_s}}{\dfrac{\Delta P}{P}}$$

The accuracy of the measure of elasticity is greater the smaller the change in price (ΔP) is. *Point elasticity* refers to the elasticity at a point on the curve where the change in price approaches zero as a limit. Calculation of the coefficient of elasticity through ordinary percentage changes is not possible in this case; calculus is necessary. (For those familiar with calculus, point elasticity at price P is equal to $dQ/dP \cdot P/Q$.)

Elasticity over a *range* in price is called *arc* elasticity, and the formula is applicable to this concept. Because elasticity normally varies from one point to another over a price range, arc elasticity is an *average*. A common way of calculating this average is to take the *midpoint* of the range in price and quantity as the base for figuring percentage changes. For example, suppose that as price changes from $1.05 to $0.95, the quantity demanded increases from 400 to 600. The percentage change in quantity is calculated as 200/500 = 40 percent, and the percentage change in price as 10/100 = 10 percent, so that the arc elasticity is 40/10 = 4. The same procedure is followed in calculating the arc elasticity of supply.

(NOTE: The sign of the coefficient of elasticity of demand—*negative,* since quantity and price change in opposite directions—is conventionally ignored. The sign for the elasticity of supply is usually positive.)

An elasticity coefficient of unity—indicating equal percentage changes in quantity and price—is the dividing line between relatively *elastic* (coefficient greater than 1) and relatively *inelastic* (coefficient less than 1) demand or supply. Over any range in price where the relative change in quantity exceeds the relative change in price, the schedule, or curve, is relatively elastic. In the contrary case, the schedule is relatively inelastic over that range. ⌣

The extremes of *zero* elasticity and *infinite* elasticity are shown graphically as vertical and horizontal curves, respectively. Thus, in Figure 12.2, *ZZ* is zero elastic throughout its length, for no change in quantity (demanded or supplied, depending upon whether the curve represents demand or supply) occurs in response to a change in price.

VV, on the other hand, is an infinitely elastic curve since any change in price from *OV* results in the complete disappearance of quantity (demanded or supplied).

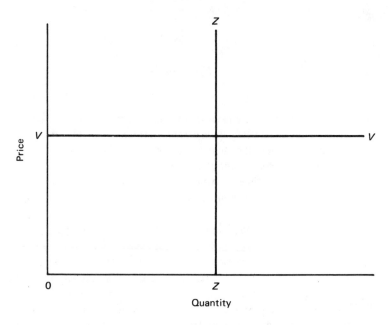

FIGURE 12.2   Zero Elastic and Infinitely Elastic Curves

c. An important aspect of the elasticity of demand is its influence on the *total expenditure* for a good at different prices. The effect of price changes on expenditure also provides a convenient *test of elasticity of demand.*

If demand over any given price range is elastic (greater than 1), total expenditure on the good varies *inversely* with a change in price—*i.e.,* expenditure increases as price falls, and decreases as price rises. If demand is inelastic (less than 1), expenditure and price move in the *same direction*—as price falls, expenditure decreases; as price rises, expenditure increases. If demand is unit elastic, total expenditure remains *constant* as price changes.

C   DISCUSSION

1   The Law of Supply and Demand

In a competitive market, the price of a good tends toward its *equilibrium level,* where the quantity of the good demanded equals the quantity supplied; at any other price, an *excess* of either the quantity demanded or quantity supplied pulls the price up or down.

For example, in Figure 12.3, at price OP_a there is *excess supply* of *LM.* This means that sellers are offering for sale *LM* more of the good than buyers are willing to purchase. To rid themselves of unsold amounts of the good, sellers *lower* the price.

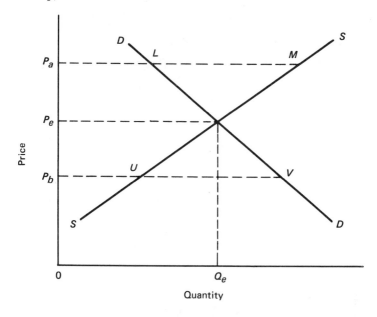

FIGURE 12.3 Equilibrium Price

At price OP_b, there is *excess demand* of *UV.* Buyers wish to purchase *UV* more of the good than sellers are offering for sale at that price. Competitive bidding among purchasers forces the price upward. At the equilibrium price OP_e, the quantity demanded is OQ_e, exactly equal to the quantity supplied. No downward or upward pressure on price is exerted, so that it remains at OP_e. This is why it is called an *equilibrium* price.

2   Changes in Equilibrium Price

A change in supply or demand ordinarily causes the equilibrium price to change; excess demand or supply now exists at the former equilibrium. For example, in Figure 12.4 let $D_1 D_1$ be the original demand curve, with the equilibrium price OP_1. Suppose that demand increases to $D_2 D_2$. At the original price OP_1 there is now *excess demand* of *UV*. Competitive bidding forces price upward until the excess demand is eliminated, namely at price OP_2.

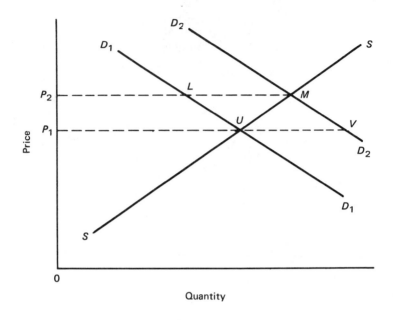

FIGURE 12.4 Change in Demand and Price

If demand had originally been $D_2 D_2$ and price OP_2, a decrease in demand to $D_1 D_1$ would have caused price to fall to OP_1, and at OP_2 there would be excess supply of *LM*.

3   Elasticity and Price-Quantity Changes

The influence of price-elasticity on relative price and quantity changes in response to a change in supply or demand is illustrated in two extreme cases in Figure 12.5 and Figure 12.6.

In the first figure, the supply curve *QS* is drawn with a zero elasticity throughout its length. In this case a shift in demand affects only price, the quantity purchased remaining constant at *OQ*.

The second figure illustrates the opposite situation. The supply curve *PS* is shown to be infinitely elastic. A shift in demand in this case has no effect on price, with the full impact falling on the quantity purchased.

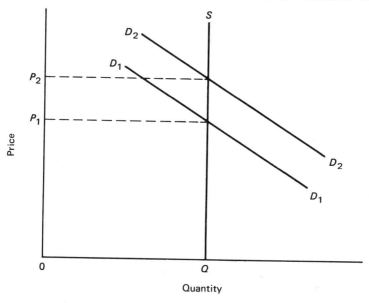

FIGURE 12.5 Change in Demand with Zero Elastic Supply

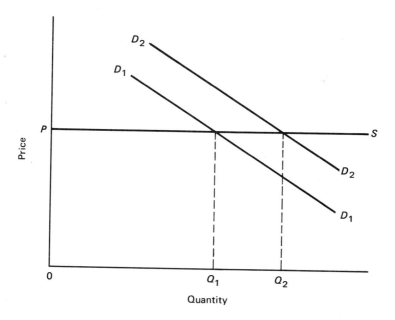

FIGURE 12.6 Change in Demand with Infinitely Elastic Supply

The same results are produced by shifts in supply under the same assumptions about the elasticity of demand. The student is encouraged to illustrate this for himself.

In the usual case, a change in demand or supply causes both a *price* and a *quantity* response: the greater the relative magnitude of price change compared to quantity, the lower the price-elasticities of the curve.

D   CONFUSIONS TO AVOID

1   Demand (Supply) versus Quantity Demanded (Supplied)

A change in demand or supply causes price to change, while changes in quantities demanded or supplied are the *result* of a price change. This points up the importance of clearly distinguishing between the two kinds of changes.

If demand increases, price rises (unless the elasticity of supply is infinite). As a result, the *quantity supplied* increases. But the latter does *not* cause price to fall back toward its original level, as would an increase in supply.

2   Elasticity and the Slope of a Demand or Supply Curve

The slope of a curve is not a measure of its elasticity. The *slope* of a demand or supply curve measures the *absolute* price-quantity ratio, while elasticity refers to *relative* ratios.

(NOTE: The slope of a demand or supply curve would be an accurate measure of the elasticity of the curve if *ratio,* or *logarithmic,* scales were used. Usually, however, price and quantity axes are laid off on *arithmetic* scales.)

CHAPTER 13 THEORY OF CONSUMER DEMAND

A PRINCIPLES

1 Shape and Position of Demand Curves

The theory of consumer demand seeks to explain the *shape* and *elasticity* of the normal demand curve and its *position.*

2 Law of Diminishing Marginal Utility

The *shape* of a demand curve reflects the relationship between the price of a good and the quantity of the good demanded.

Normally, the quantity of a good demanded varies *inversely* with its price, yielding a *demand curve* that falls from left to right on the conventional diagram.

The underlying explanation of the shape of the demand curve is the law of *Diminishing Marginal Utility.* An alternative, though consistent, explanation is in terms of the *substitution* and *income* effects.

3 The Price-Elasticity of Demand

The price-elasticity of demand—that is, the relative change in quantity demanded compared to a relative change in price—is determined mainly by the number of close substitute goods available, the extent to which the good is regarded as a necessity, and the importance of the good in consumer budgets. Elasticity is greater the:

102 / Price Theory

greater the number of close substitutes,
less the good is regarded as a necessity, and
greater the portion of budgets spent on the good.

4 Position of and Changes in Demand

a. The magnitude of demand for a good depends mainly upon *disposable personal income*, the *prices* of *substitute and complementary* goods, tastes or preferences, and *expectations* of future *price and availability* of the good.

Demand tends to be greater the larger the disposable income, the higher the price of substitute goods and the lower the price of complementary goods, the greater the preferences for the good, and the greater the expectations of future higher prices or shortages of the good.

b. A given demand curve is based on given levels of disposable income, prices of other goods, tastes, and expectations.

A change in demand is caused by a change in any one of a number of variables:

1. demand normally changes in the same direction as a change in disposable income and is measured by the *income-elasticity* of demand,
2. demand shifts in the *same* direction as changes in the prices of close *substitutes*, and in the *opposite* direction from changes in the prices of *complementary* goods,
3. a change in tastes for a good causes the demand for it to change in the *same* direction, and
4. an expected future decrease in availability or an increase in the price of a good causes the demand for it to rise; contrary expectations cause demand to fall.

B CONCEPTS

1 The Law of Diminishing Marginal Utility

This "law" states that, other things being equal, the greater the quantity of a good is one's possession, the less additional utility is yielded by an extra unit of the good. *Utility* means the *want-satisfying power* of a good, or simply the personal satisfaction yielded by it.

The term *marginal* means *additional* or *extra.* Marginal utility, therefore, refers to the additional satisfaction obtained from possessing one more unit of a good.

2   Substitution and Income Effects

    a. When the price of a good changes, the prices of other goods remaining the same, there is a tendency for consumers to switch the pattern of their expenditure; the good or goods whose relative price has fallen is substituted for the good or goods the relative price of which has risen. This is called the *substitution* effect.

    b. Other things being equal, when the price of a good changes, the *real income* (the purchasing power of money income) of consumers changes in the *opposite* direction. Thus, if the price of a good falls, the ability of consumers to purchase it increases; if the price rises, this ability is reduced. This is called the *income effect* of a price change.

3   Substitute and Complementary Goods

    Goods are classified as substitute, complementary, and unrelated. Butter and margarine are substitute goods, phonographs and records are complementary, hamburger and shirts are unrelated.

4   Income-Elasticity of Demand

    The *price-elasticity* of demand measures the degree of responsiveness of quantity demanded to a *price* change. The *income-elasticity* of demand measures the degree of responsiveness of demand (that is, the whole schedule or curve) to a change in *income.*

    The coefficient of the income-elasticity of demand is equal to the percentage change in quantity demanded at each price, divided by the percentage change in income. Except for so-called inferior goods, the sign of the coefficient of income-elasticity is positive, though its numerical value varies widely among different goods.

C   DISCUSSION

1   The Left-to-Right Decline of the Demand Curve

    a. Given unchanged money income, prices of other goods, tastes, and expectations (all held constant in constructing the demand for a good), the demand curve for a particular good normally falls from left to right (see Figure 11.1, p. 87) because of the law of Diminishing Marginal Utility, in conjunction with the postulate of *rational economic behavior.* This postulate states that consumers attempt to *maximize* the *total utility* obtainable from a given amount of expenditure. To accomplish this goal, the *marginal utility* yielded by the *last dollar* spent on every good purchased must be the *same.*

If, for example, the marginal utility obtained by a consumer from the hundredth dollar spent on hamburger (say over a year's period) is less than that obtained from the fiftieth dollar spent on steaks, the consumer can increase his *total utility*—without changing his total expenditure—by purchasing *less* hamburger and *more* steaks. As the consumption of steaks increases and that of hamburger decreases, the marginal utility of the former decreases and of the latter increases—a result following from the law of Diminishing Marginal Utility. When the marginal utility of the last dollar spent is the same for both goods (and all other goods purchased), total utility is *maximized,* for no further improvement is possible.

The principle for maximizing utility for all goods purchased by the consumer, where *MU* represents marginal utility, the subscript the good, and *P* the price, can be formally expressed as:

$$\frac{MU_X}{P_X} = \frac{MU_Y}{P_Y} = \frac{MU_Z}{P_Z} \quad \cdots$$

In constructing the demand curve for good *X,* the prices of other goods (say *Y* and *Z*) are held constant. How much *X* is demanded at any given price is then determined by fulfilling the maximization condition stated in the formula. Now suppose that the price of *X* falls. At the lower price, a dollar will buy a greater quantity, so that the marginal utility of a dollar's worth of *X* will be greater than before. To bring the marginal utility of a dollar's worth of *X* back into equality with the marginal utility of a dollar's worth of *Y, Z,* and other goods, a greater quantity of *X* is purchased. That is, at a lower price the quantity of *X* demanded is greater—precisely what the left-to-right decline in the demand curve indicates.

b. Explanation of the declining demand curve can also be approached, without specific reference to diminishing marginal utility, through the *substitution* and *income* effects of a price change. As the price of a good falls, other prices remaining constant, consumers tend to substitute that good for others in their purchases. (This will be explained further in connection with the price-elasticity of demand.)

In addition, the effect of the lower price in raising the real income of the consumer may induce greater purchases of the good. For both these reasons, the demand curve for a good falls from left to right.

2 Determinants of Price-Elasticity of Demand

The *price-elasticity* of demand is largely determined by the extent and degree to which there are substitute relations among goods. Since butter and margarine are very close substitutes, a decrease in the price of either, the other's price remaining constant, will cause a larger increase in the quantity demanded— *i.e.,* a greater elasticity of demand—than would be the case if they were not so closely substitutable. Goods for which there are no good substitutes (such as certain medicines, to take an extreme example) generally have a very *low elasticity* of demand.

Besides substitutability, price-elasticity of demand is influenced by the nature of the good and its importance in consumer budgets. The demand for basic foodstuffs is usually inelastic, simply because minimum amounts must be purchased regardless of price. Since a "luxury" good can be dispensed with, the quantity demanded tends to be responsive to price. Likewise, if expenditure on a good is a significant part of consumer budgets, demand tends to be elastic because a change in price has a noticeable impact on budgets. But for a commodity like salt, the expenditure for which has little significance for budgets, the demand is highly inelastic.

3 Determinants of Demand and Changes in Demand

That demand for a good should depend upon income, prices of substitute and complementary goods, tastes, and expectations can easily be shown.

a. Income is limited, reflecting economic scarcity. Limited income constitutes a *budget constraint* on purchases. While it is possible for individual consumers to spend more than their disposable income (through borrowing, dissaving, etc.), real income generally places an upper limit on consumption expenditure. For the economy as a whole, this limit is rarely reached because of the desire to save some portion of income.

   The normal effect of a change in disposable income is for a corresponding change, fractionally smaller, in consumer expenditure. (For this, the *consumption function,* see Chapter 2.) The change in consumer expenditure is not spread evenly over all goods, but weighted in favor of those goods for which the *income-elasticity* of demand is highest.

b. The demand for a good is affected by the prices of substitute goods because of the possibility of switching purchases. If the price of margarine falls, the demand for butter *decreases,* since some consumers at least will switch from butter to margarine. (Note that the elasticity of demand is also high because of this substitutability.) Conversely, a rise in the price of margarine causes an *increase* in the demand for butter.

The relationship for complementary goods is the *opposite* of that for substitute goods. If the price of phonographs falls, and therefore the quantity demanded increases, the demand for records is likely to increase.

(NOTE: A technical way of identifying substitute and complementary relationships is through the sign of the *cross-elasticity* of demand. This is defined as the percentage change in the quantity of a good demanded, divided by the percentage change in the price of *another* good. If the sign is *positive*, the goods are *substitutes*; if it is *negative*, they are *complementary*.)

c. The role of *taste* in determining demand is obvious. If consumer preferences turn in favor of a particular good, the demand for it increases; if the good falls out of favor, the demand for it decreases.

d. *Expectations* influence demand, especially for those goods which can easily be stored and the consumption of which can be postponed, as is the case for most durable goods. If a good is expected to become in short supply or to rise in price, the demand for it increases as consumers attempt to avoid having to do without it or paying a higher price later. Opposite expectations induce the postponement of purchases and a decrease in present demand.

D CONFUSIONS TO AVOID

1 Changes in Demand and in Quantity Demanded

This vital distinction was discussed in Chapter 12: a change in demand occurs as a result of change in one or more of the variables held *constant* in constructing a given demand curve—namely, income, prices of other goods, tastes, and expectations. A change in quantity demanded occurs as a result of a change in the price of the good. While a change in demand involves a *shift* in the entire curve, a change in quantity demanded involves only a movement along a given curve.

2 Marginal and Total Utility

As long as marginal utility is greater than zero, *total* utility increases even if marginal utility is declining, since marginal utility is the *addition* to total utility.

3 Maximization of Utility

Avoid the pitfall of thinking that the marginal utility of all goods purchased should be equalized to maximize utility. The maximization rule is the equalization of the marginal utility *per dollar's worth* of different goods.

4 The Role of Substitutability

The presence of close substitutability among goods has two different aspects: it contributes to the price-elasticity of demand, and it is a source of changes in demand. The demand for butter is more elastic because of the availability of margarine. The demand for butter changes if the price of margarine changes. The first effect influences the *shape* of the demand curve, the second the *position* of the demand curve.

CHAPTER **14** THE THEORY OF COMPETITIVE SUPPLY

A PRINCIPLES

1 Market Supply

The *market supply* of a good is the sum of the quantities offered for sale at different unit prices by all the firms in the industry.

2 Supply and Profits

The supply of a good offered on the market by a firm is determined by the efforts of the firm to *maximize its profits.* Profits are maximized when *marginal costs are equated with marginal revenue.*

3 Short-Run Competitive Supply

In the short run, a competitive firm maximizes its profits by producing at the output where *marginal costs* of production equal the *market price* of the good. Hence, the market short-run supply curve under pure competition is the sum of the marginal cost curves of the firms in the industry.

(Qualification: a firm will not produce at all if market price is not at least as great as the firm's *average variable costs* of production.)

4 Long-Run Competitive Supply

In the long run, the competitive supply price of a good is equal to both marginal costs and to the *lowest* long-run average costs of production. Therefore, the long-run supply curve is the sum of those outputs of firms in the industry at which long-run average costs are at a minimum.

B CONCEPTS

1 Profits

Profits (π) are the difference between total revenue (TR) and total costs (TC):

$$\pi = TR - TC$$

Included in costs are *all expenses* of production, both *implicit* and *explicit.* An *explicit* cost involves an actual money outlay by the firm, as for wage payments, raw materials, etc. An *implicit* cost is not accompanied by an actual payment, but would necessitate a payment if the firm did not itself own the resource used in production. If a firm borrows money, interest payments on the loan are an explicit cost; but if the firm uses its own funds there is an implicit interest cost equivalent to the cost of borrowed money. Other examples of implicit costs include the rental value of owned buildings and land and the wages for the managerial services of owners of the firm.

2 Marginal Costs

Marginal costs are the extra, or additional, costs incurred in producing one more unit of a good. They are measured by the *difference* in total costs per extra unit produced.

Example: if the total cost of 100 units of output is $100 and of 101 units $102, marginal costs over this range of output are $2.

In symbolic language, letting MC represent marginal costs, TC total costs, Q output, and Δ change:

$$MC = \frac{\Delta(TC)}{\Delta Q}$$

3 Marginal Revenue

Marginal revenue is the extra, or additional, revenue obtained from selling one more unit of a good. It is measured by the *difference* in total revenue per extra unit of sale.

Example: If 10 units can be sold at 10 cents per unit, and 12 units at 9 cents per unit, marginal revenue over this range is 4 cents. Calculation:

Total revenue at 10 cents	=	$1.00
Total revenue at 9 cents	=	1.08
Difference in revenue	=	$0.08
Extra units sold	=	2
Extra revenue per unit	=	$0.04

In symbols, letting *MR* represent marginal revenue, *TR* total revenue, and *Q* sales (or output):

$$MR = \frac{\Delta(TR)}{\Delta Q}$$

4 The Short and Long Run

The *short run* is defined as the period during which a firm is unable to expand its productive capacity by adding to its plant and equipment. Output can be varied only through the more or less intensive use of *existing* plant and equipment.

During the *long run,* plant and equipment can be enlarged—or depreciated out of existence (that is, used up without replacement). Thus, output can be increased in the long run through the expansion of productive capacity. Also, the *industry's* output in the long run can be increased through the entry of additional firms into the industry.

5 Fixed, Variable, and Average Costs

Fixed costs—distinguished from *variable* costs—are costs which remain at a given level regardless of output. *Variable* costs are those which vary with the level of output.

In the *short run,* some costs are fixed, others variable. In the *long run, all* costs are *variable.*

Total costs are fixed plus variable costs. *Average* costs are costs per unit of output. *Average fixed costs* are fixed costs per unit of output; *average variable costs* are variable costs per unit of output. Average *total* costs are total costs (fixed plus variable) per unit of output. *Marginal* costs are *unaffected* by *fixed* costs.

C   DISCUSSION

1   Rule for Profit Maximization

Profits are maximized when marginal revenue (*MR*) equals marginal costs (*MC*); if these are not equal, profits can be increased by changing output until equality is established. Suppose at the present output and sales of a firm, marginal revenue is $1.00 and marginal costs $0.75. If one more unit of output is produced, total costs increase by $0.75, total revenue by $1.00, thus total profits by $0.25. Or suppose that at a given output and sales volume, marginal revenue is $1.00 and marginal costs $1.15. If one unit *less* of output is produced, total revenue falls by $1.00, total costs decline by $1.15, and total profits increase by $0.15. If, however, marginal revenue and marginal costs are each $1.00, no increase in profits is possible through changing the level of output.

2   Short-Run Supply

In pure competition, the *market price* of a good is the same as the individual firm's *marginal revenue*, since in such a case there are so many firms in an industry that no single firm's output has an appreciable influence on market price. If the market price is $1.00, for example, the individual firm adds $1.00 to its total revenue from the sale of an extra unit of the good, no matter how many additional units it offers for sales. Therefore, in following the maximum-profit rule (*MR* = *MC*), each firm equates market price with marginal costs. This yields a *supply curve* for each firm identical with its *marginal cost curve*. Figure 14.1 shows this, where *MC* is the marginal cost curve of a firm, *P* the market price of the good, *Q* the firm's output. If the market price is OP_1, the firm produces and offers for sale OQ_1 quantity; at price OP_2, OQ_2 quantity; and at price OP_3, OQ_3 quantity.

The *total* supply of the good is equal to the *sum* of the supplies offered by the firms in the industry. Thus, the total supply curve is equal to the (horizontal) sum of the marginal cost curves of the firms in the industry.

(An exception to this would occur if the market price were too low to cover the firm's *average variable costs.* In this case, it pays the firm to *shut down* and produce *nothing*. *Fixed* costs are not relevant to the firm's decisions in the short run, since, by definition, such costs are incurred regardless of output.)

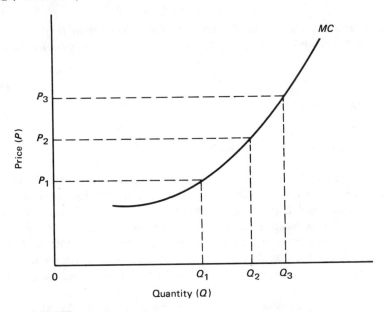

FIGURE 14.1 Short-Run Competitive Supply

3 Long-Run Supply

The competitive equilibrium supply price in the long run is equal to long-run *marginal costs* and also to the *lowest* long-run *average costs* of firms in the industry. Each firm assures equality between price and marginal costs in following the maximum-profit rule.

Equality between price and long-run *average* costs is brought about through *freedom of entry* into competitive industries. If price were *above* average costs, excess (or "economic") profits would be realized, inducing additional firms to enter the industry. The greater number of firms would increase the market supply, forcing the price downward. If price were *below* average costs, firms would suffer *losses*, inducing some firms to leave the industry. This would reduce market supply and force the price upward.

Hence, in *long-run competitive equilibrium,* the *price* of a *good* is that just *equal* to the *average costs of producing* it.

When price is equal to both *average costs* and *marginal costs,* average costs must be at their *minimum* level. Average and marginal measures are so related that when the average is rising, the marginal value must be *greater* than the average; when the average is falling, the marginal value must be *less* than the average; and when the average is neither rising nor falling, the marginal value must be *equal* to it.

But if the average is neither rising nor falling, it must be either at a *maximum* or *minimum.* For reasons explained in the next chapter, long-run average costs in equilibrium must be at a minimum point. Therefore equality between marginal and average costs implies that average costs are at a minimum.

D CONFUSIONS TO AVOID

1 "Economic" Compared to "Business" Profits

In the business world, only *explicit* costs are usually deducted from the firm's revenue to arrive at profits. But in an economic sense, the market values of owned resource services should be counted as a cost, for they represent foregone opportunities—the essential nature of economic cost. Thus, a firm which uses its own money capital in the business gives up the opportunity of earning interest through lending in the market.

For a firm to remain in business over the long run, it need earn no economic profits, for zero economic profits yield normal returns on invested capital. In short, zero economic profits are equivalent to the business concept of "normal" profits.

2 Maximum Profits and Absolute Profits

The maximum-profit rule, $MR = MC,$ does not indicate the actual level of profits. It only states the condition necessary for profits to be maximized, whatever their amount. Indeed, in the short run, a firm may be unable to avoid losing money. In this case, it seeks to minimize its losses. To do this, it follows the rule for maximum profits, namely, equalizing marginal revenue and marginal costs.

3 Short- and Long-Run Equilibrium

The supply of a good is dependent upon two variables:

>   the output at various prices of each firm, and
>   the number of firms in the industry.

The output of each firm is based upon its efforts to maximize profits, or, if losses are unavoidable, to minimize the losses. Provided there are no serious barriers to entry into the industry, the number of firms is based on the present and prospective future rate of return on investments in that industry. Under competitive conditions, with barriers to entry low, new firms are attracted into industries where economic profits exist—*i.e.,* where business profits are above normal—and firms leave industries where economic losses are being incurred.

In the short run, supply is determined entirely by the decisions of existing firms, since new firms cannot be established. Therefore, the short-run equilibrium price may yield positive or negative economic profits. In the long run, economic profits tend to be zero, the condition for stability in the number of firms in the industry and in the supply of the good.

CHAPTER 15 PRODUCTIVITY AND COSTS

A PRINCIPLES

1 Productivity, Costs, and Supply

Supply depends upon the costs of production, which in turn depend upon the *productivity* and *prices* of the inputs used in the production process.

2 The Production Function

The productivity of inputs behaves according to the laws of production, reflected in the *production function.*

3 The Law of Variable Proportions

In the usual case, a given output can be produced with different input combinations—*i.e.,* inputs can be substituted for one another, within limits, in producing a given output.

As the proportion of one input over other inputs is increased, the marginal product of the increased input eventually decreases. This is known as the law of *Variable Proportions,* or *Diminishing Returns.*

4 Returns to Scale

If all inputs are increased in the *same* proportion, a firm's output responds according to the laws of scale. With *constant* returns to scale, output increases in the *same* proportion as all inputs are increased. With *increasing* returns to scale, output increases in a *greater* proportion than inputs; with *decreasing* returns to scale output increases proportionately *less* than inputs.

5 Productivity and Costs

If input (factor) prices are given to the individual firm and unaffected by the quantity it employs, *average variable* and *marginal costs of production* are the inverse of the average and marginal products, respectively, of variable inputs.

6 Short-Run Costs and Supply

In the short run, because of the law of Variable Proportions, the average and marginal products of variable inputs decrease beyond a certain output level; this is accompanied by increasing average variable and marginal costs. Hence, since short-run competitive supply is equivalent to the sum of the marginal cost curves of firms in the industry, the short-run supply curve rises from left to right, under pure competition.

7 Long-Run Productivity and Costs

With constant returns to scale, average and marginal products of inputs remain constant at different levels of output, with average and marginal costs also remaining constant and equal to each other. With increasing returns to scale, average and marginal products rise as the scale of output increases, leading to decreasing average costs and marginal costs lower than average costs.

With decreasing returns to scale, average and marginal products fall as the scale of output increases, causing increasing average and marginal costs, with the latter greater than average costs.

Typically, the long-run average cost curve is either horizontal to near-capacity output (reflecting constant returns to scale), thereafter rising (reflecting decreasing returns to scale); or it falls in early stages (reflecting increasing returns to scale), reaching a minimum (where returns to scale are constant), and thereafter rising (after decreasing returns to scale set in). Correspondingly, the long-run marginal cost curve typically is either horizontal to near-capacity output and then rises; or it falls, reaches a minimum, and thereafter rises.

These prototypes of long-run cost curves are illustrated in Figure 15.1, (a) and (b).

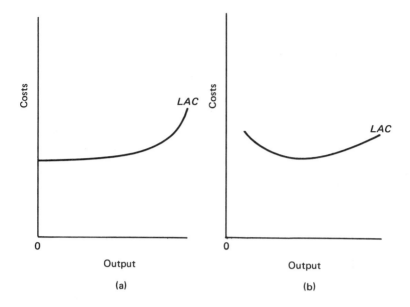

FIGURE 15.1   Long-Run Cost Curves

8   Long-Run Competitive Supply Curve

In pure competition, each firm in the long run tends to produce at its minimum long-run average cost point. The long-run supply curve, therefore, is based on the minimum average costs of production at different levels of the industry's output.

The long-run supply curve is horizontal, rises from left to right, or falls from left to right, accordingly as long-run average cost curves respectively remain stationary, move up, or move down as the number of firms in the industry increases.

Industries in these respective conditions are called constant-cost, increasing, and decreasing-cost. Constant-cost conditions are usually found in relatively small industries which employ negligible proportions of the total supplies of inputs. Increasing-cost conditions are the norm for large industries employing a significant fraction of the total supply of one or more inputs, or where there are external diseconomies of scale. Decreasing-cost conditions are present when there are external economies of scale.

9   Least-Cost Combination of Inputs

Each cost curve, short- and long-run, is based on the presumption that every firm always produces any given output at the least possible cost. This is accomplished by combining inputs in such proportions that the marginal product per dollar's amount of input is the same for all inputs. Symbolically stated, the cost of any given output is minimized when

$$\frac{MPP_a}{W_a} = \frac{MPP_b}{W_b} = \frac{MPP_c}{W_c} = \ldots$$

where *MPP* represents marginal physical product, *W* the price per unit of input, and the subscripts *a, b, c,* represent particular inputs.

B CONCEPTS

1 The Production Function

The production function is the underlying determinant of the shape of cost curves. It is a purely technical relationship between inputs and output, having, as such, no economic foundations but profound economic consequences. The function shows what different kinds of inputs, combined in a variety of ways, will yield in various amounts of output.

The two most important "laws" the production function obeys are the law of *Variable Proportions* (or Diminishing Returns) and of *Returns to Scale*; the first law is applicable when the proportion among inputs is varied; the second when the proportion among inputs is held constant.

2 Average and Marginal Products

The *average product* of an input is the amount of output per unit of input. It is found by dividing total output by the number of units of the input.

Marginal product is the additional or extra output resulting from adding one more unit of an input to given quantities of other inputs.

It should be noted that these concepts are exactly parallel with those of average and marginal costs (see Chapter 14).

3 Fixed and Variable Inputs

As the names imply, a *fixed* input is one which remains constant in quantity, even though output changes, while a *variable* input is one whose amount changes with differences in output. Fixed inputs involve fixed costs; variable inputs are responsible for variable costs.

4 Internal and External Economies and Diseconomies of Scale

An *internal economy of scale* is an economy arising out of the scale of operation of the individual firm. An *external economy of scale* is one arising out of the scale of operation of the whole industry. These distinctions apply in the same way to internal and external *diseconomies*.

C DISCUSSION

1 The Law of Variable Proportions

In some cases, the output of a product requires the use of specified inputs in a fixed proportion. For example, to produce one unit of good X may necessitate the employment of five units of input A, plus eight units of input B, no other combination being technically feasible. In such cases the law of Variable Proportions is not applicable.

More usually, however, different kinds of input may be combined in a variety of ways to yield the same given output. Among other considerations, this gives rise to the question of what is the economically best combination to employ (see p. 123).

When the proportion of one input to other inputs is changed, the marginal product of the increased input eventually decreases. The simplest example of this, the law of Variable Proportions, is where all inputs but one are held constant—say land and capital—with varying amounts of labor employed in producing some crop (say wheat) with the following relationships:

Units of Labor (man-years)	Total Output (in bushels)	Average Product of Labor (in bushels)	Marginal Product of Labor (in bushels)
0	0	0	0
1	500	500	500
2	1200	600	700
3	1800	600	600
4	2300	575	500
5	2500	500	200

In this example, diminishing returns set in after the second unit of labor is applied to the fixed amount of land and capital, as evidenced by the decreasing marginal product beginning with the third man-year of labor.

The amount of land and capital available per man-year decreases as the number of man-years of labor increases. The average and marginal product of labor decreases after any advantages of the division of labor are gained. The phenomenon of diminishing returns grows out of the reduced quantities of other inputs with which each unit of an increased input has to work.

2 Returns to Scale

Increasing returns to scale (sometimes called *internal economies* of scale) are attributable to the efficiencies arising out of more extensive specialization of productive resources and to the so-called "indivisibilities" of certain resources.

A large-scale operation may generate economies—which are not feasible on a reduced scale—through the advantages of specialization permitted by such techniques as assembly-line production.

Indivisibilities are a related cause of internal economies of scale. An input resource is said to be indivisible if it cannot be duplicated on a smaller scale without loss of productive efficiency. For example, a million-dollar metal-stamping machine may have a daily capacity output of 500 automobile fenders. From an engineering standpoint, it will probably not be feasible to fabricate a machine with an output capacity of 250 fenders and costing a half-million dollars, and still less a machine with a capacity of 50 fenders and costing $100 thousand. In such cases a minimum scale of operations is required to meet the ultimate efficiency of the equipment. Until that scale is reached, average costs decline as the scale of operations expands.

Decreasing returns to scale (*internal diseconomies of scale*) are usually attributable to the difficulties of management after a firm reaches a certain critical size. Eventually the economies of scale are all exhausted, and efficient management becomes increasingly difficult. As managerial inefficiencies creep in, average costs begin to climb.

3 Productivity and Costs

Productivity and variable *costs* are inversely proportional if the prices of inputs remain constant. Suppose that the wage rate is $20 per day. If the output per worker (the average product of labor) is give units, the labor cost per unit of produce is $4; if the average product is ten units, the labor cost is $2, etc.

The same inverse relationship holds for *marginal product* and *marginal cost*. If a worker is added to the labor force, the firm's costs rise by the amount of wages paid him—$20 a day. If the extra worker adds four units to total output (his marginal product), marginal costs are $5; if his marginal product were eight units, marginal costs would be $2.50, etc.

4 Short-Run Costs

The short-run average variable cost (*AVC*) curve of a firm is U-shaped, as shown in Figure 15.2. The marginal cost (*MC*) curve has a similar shape. (Average and marginal values are related to each other in a definite way.)

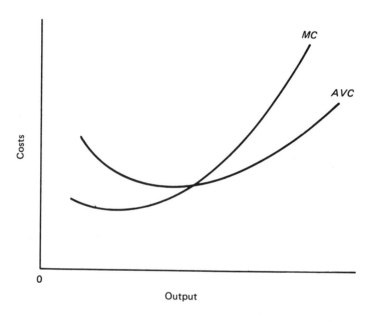

FIGURE 15.2 **Average Variable and Marginal Cost Curves**

The shape of these cost curves is merely a reflection of the behavior of the *average* and *marginal products* of the variable inputs. (*Fixed* inputs do not influence variable or marginal costs.) As output increases, at first average and marginal products *increase,* causing average and marginal costs to *decline.* Increasing productivity in this early stage is created by the more efficient operation of the firm as it moves toward an optimum relationship between variable and fixed inputs. At some output level, however, diminishing returns set in, since the proportion of variable to fixed inputs increases as output expands. When *marginal* diminishing returns set in and the marginal product begins to fall, marginal costs begin to rise. Somewhat later, *average* diminishing returns occur, the average product falls, and average costs rise.

(NOTE: Average fixed costs are fixed costs per unit of output—*i.e.,* total fixed costs divided by total output. The average fixed cost curve falls from left to right, with the rate of decline proportional to the increase in output—if output doubles, average fixed costs halve, etc. Fixed costs do not affect production decisions in the short run, since nothing can be done about them. But they do affect the total profits or losses of a firm. If total costs, including fixed as well as variable costs, are not covered by revenue, in the *long run* a firm will be forced to close down.)

5 Long-Run Costs

As for short-run cost curves, the shape of long-run cost curves depend upon the productivity of inputs (see Figure 15.1). However, productivity follows the laws of returns to scale, since all inputs can be increased in the same proportions.

An infinitely elastic (horizontal) long-run average cost curve is the counterpart of *constant* average products. If all inputs were doubled or tripled, total output correspondingly doubled or tripled, the cost per unit of output would remain constant. When average costs are constant, marginal costs must be equal to average costs, so marginal costs, too, are constant in this case.

If the long-run average cost curve has a section that falls from left to right, this results from increasing average productivity as output expands. If, as inputs were all doubled in amount, total output tripled, the costs per unit of output obviously would fall. And when average costs are falling, marginal costs must be less than average.

The upturning section of the long-run average cost curve reflects decreasing average products. If as all inputs were increased by 10 percent, total output increased by only 5 percent, the costs per unit of output would necessarily rise, and marginal costs would have to lie above average costs.

In summary, to the extent that a firm benefits from *internal economies of scale* over a range of output, the average cost curve falls from left to right. When internal *diseconomies* of scale begin to operate, the average cost curve rises from left to right. Over any range of output where *constant* returns to scale prevail, the average cost curve is horizontal.

6 Costs and Supply

a. In Chapter 14 it was shown that the competitive short-run supply curve of a good is equivalent to the horizontal sum of the marginal cost curves of firms in the industry. The basic reason for upsloping market supply curves in the short run is now apparent: marginal cost curves rise from left to right because the marginal products of variable inputs decline in response to diminishing returns—the law of Variable Proportions.

b. It was also shown in the preceding chapter that the long-run competitive supply price of a good is equal in equilibrium to the lowest average costs of production. The question, then, is what happens to the position of firms' long-run cost curves as the industry expands.

As long as the prices of inputs to firms and the productivity of their inputs are unaffected by the number of firms in the industry, the position of their average cost curves is unaffected by the size of the industry. The minimum average costs of production remain constant over different industry output levels and the long-run supply curve is horizontal—it is a *constant-cost* industry.

If, however, either the prices of inputs increase to firms or the productivity of inputs decline as the industry expands, average cost curves are displaced in an upward direction, with minimum average costs higher at greater industry output levels. In such an *increasing-cost* industry, the long-run supply curve slopes upward from left to right. Increased input prices are likely to result if industry's demand is sufficiently great to affect input market prices. Decreasing productivity of inputs may be attributable to external diseconomies of scale.

It is possible for average cost curves to move vertically downward as an industry expands because of external economies of scale, such as those arising from a better-trained supply of labor. In this case, minimum average costs fall as the industry's output increases, and the long-run supply curve falls from left to right—a *decreasing-cost* industry.

7 Least-Cost Input Combination

The rule for the *least-cost* combination of inputs can be shown by a simple example. Assume that a firm employs two inputs, A and B. Suppose that the per unit price of A is $10 and of B $20. With some particular combination of A and B, let the marginal product of A be five units of output and of B twenty units of output. In this case the least-cost rule of equalizing the marginal product per dollar's amount of inputs is violated, since $5/10 \neq 20/20$. If the firm were to substitute input B for input A while keeping output constant, only one-fourth unit of B is required to replace one unit of A, since the marginal product of B is four times that of A. But giving up one unit of A saves the firm $10, while hiring an extra quarter-unit of B adds only $5 to costs. The firm thus reduces its total costs by a net amount of $5.

The substitution of B for A continues to lower costs until, as a result of diminishing returns, the marginal product of B falls and of A rises to the point where there is *equality* in the ratios of marginal products to input prices. Thereafter, further cost reductions are not possible through changing the input combination.

D   CONFUSIONS TO AVOID

1   Diminishing Returns and Returns to Scale

The phenomenon of diminishing returns in its most general sense occurs as a result either of changing the proportion among inputs or of internal diseconomies of scale. Historically, however, diminishing returns is associated only with the former, and this is emphasized by its modern designation as the law of Variable Proportions rather than the older law of Diminishing Returns. In any event, it is important to keep in mind the different underlying bases of diminishing returns due to varying input proportions on the one hand, and because of the scale of operations on the other hand.

2   Minimum Average Costs and Least Costs

Minimum average costs refer to the average costs incurred when a firm is producing at the lowest point of its average cost curve. Except under conditions of long-run constant returns to scale, there is one, or a limited-range, output level at which average costs are lower than at any other output level. (This is known as the *optimum* output.)

Least costs refer to an altogether different relationship. Here it is a question of incurring the least possible costs of producing *any given output*—not just the lowest average-cost output. The entire average cost curve is constructed on the assumption that least-cost input combinations are employed at each output point.

3   Long-Run Average Costs and Competitive Supply

In the short run, supply curves are the sums of marginal cost curves. In the long run, although competitive supply is related to minimum long-run average costs, the supply curve is *not* the sum of average cost curves. Rather, the long-run supply curve is derived by finding the minimum long-run average costs at various outputs of the industry. If the industry is not one of constant costs, minimum average costs vary with the industry's output. But the variations in cost do not arise out of movement along the average cost curves of firms; they arise out of the *vertical* movement of the entire cost curve of each firm in the industry.

4   Internal versus External Economies and Diseconomies

An *internal* economy or diseconomy is related to the operation of the individual firm and accounts for the shape of the firm's long-run average cost curve.

An *external* economy or diseconomy arises from forces outside the control of the individual firm and is related to the output of the industry. For example, a firm's average costs of production may rise as it increases its output because of decreasingly efficient management. This is an *internal* diseconomy and is reflected in the upward-sloping section of the firm's long-run average cost curve.

On the other hand, each firm in an industry may find its average costs of production rising at every output level as the industry's output expands as, for example, less suitable input resources are available. This is an *external* diseconomy and is reflected in the upward shift of each firm's long-run average cost curve.

CHAPTER 16 OUTPUT AND PRICE UNDER IMPERFECT COMPETITION

A PRINCIPLES

1 Types of Market

Imperfect competition embraces all market structures outside of perfect or pure competition. The principal types of imperfectly competitive sellers' markets are pure *monopoly, monopolistic competition,* and *oligopoly.*

2 Costs and Revenue

As long as imperfectly competitive firms purchase inputs in competitive markets their *costs of production,* except for *selling* costs, are subject to the same forces as competitive firms.

The chief difference between the market position of competitive and imperfectly competitive firms lies in *demand* or *revenue.* The demand for the output of an individual competitive firm is infinitely elastic at the prevailing market price, and the average and marginal revenue curves of the firm are identical; with imperfect competition the demand for the output of the individual firm slopes from left to right, and its average and marginal revenue curves are less than infinitely elastic.

3 Output and Price Under Pure Monopoly

a. A pure monopoly consists of a single firm in an industry producing a good for which there is no close substitute. Owing to the absence of close substitutes, demand for the product (and the firm's average revenue or price curve) tend to be inelastic below a certain price. The marginal revenue curve of the firm falls from left to right and is *negative* over price ranges at which the demand or average revenue curve is inelastic.

b. The monopolist's maximum-profit output is that which equalizes marginal costs and marginal revenue. Since marginal costs are always positive, this output point must lie within the elastic range of the demand curve. The output sells at a price determined by the demand curve.

c. The continued existence of pure monopoly implies closed entry into the industry; no force, as in pure competition, can eliminate the economic profits (excess business profits) of the firm.

d. Because price, or average revenue, is necessarily greater than marginal revenue when average revenue (demand) is less than infinitely elastic, a monopolistic price is greater than marginal costs. This results in restriction of output below the socially optimum level. One exception is natural monopolies subject to public regulation, as in the case of public utilities.

4 Output and Price Under Monopolistic Competition

a. Monopolistic competition consists of many firms in an industry, each producing a good which is *differentiated* from other firms; the products of the other firms, however, are considered close substitutes. Entry into the industry is relatively free.

b. Because of the differentiation of the firm's product, the demand, or average revenue, curve is less than infinitely elastic; but because of the presence of close substitutes, the demand curve tends to be elastic over normal price ranges. Correspondingly, marginal revenue tends to be positive, though always less than average revenue.

c. In order to maximize profits, the firm produces where marginal revenue and marginal costs are equal. Given this output point, the price of the product is determined by demand.

Price is necessarily above marginal costs. In the short run, price may also be above average costs and yield economic profits. But in the long run, because of freedom of entry into the industry, economic profits tend to be eliminated and price brought into equality with average as well as marginal costs. However, this occurs at an output level less than the output at which long-run average costs are at a minimum.

d. Social objections to monopolistic competition include pricing above marginal costs, production at above minimum average costs (leading to "excess capacity"), and the addition of selling costs to ordinary production costs. A possible benefit of monopolistic competition is the richer variety of products it fosters and the wider choice of products it can offer the consumer. Moreover, in many cases monopolistic competition is socially the best market structure of all those practically feasible.

5 Output and Price Under Oligopoly

a. Oligopoly is characterized by the presence of a few firms in an industry, among which there is an interdependent and rivaling relationship. If the output of different firms is standardized, there is homogeneous oligopoly; if output is differentiated, heterogeneous oligopoly. Entry into the industry is typically *restricted,* though not necessarily closed, as in pure monopoly.

b. Although the demand (average revenue) curve of an oligopolistic firm falls from left to right, in the absence of agreement among the firms the elasticity of the curve is uncertain. The result of a change in price by one firm depends upon not only the elasticity of demand for the industry's product, but also upon the reactions of other firms in the industry. As a consequence, price wars and "kinked" demand curves (accompanied by discontinuous marginal revenue curves) are characteristic of noncollusive oligopoly.

c. Because of the interdependence and uncertainty of oligopolistic firms there is a strong tendency for them to arrive at some agreement or understanding to pursue policies in the common interest or to avoid conflicting policies.

With explicit agreements (such as *cartels*) outlawed by antitrust laws, other, less formal, techniques of cooperation have evolved. The most common of these are *price leadership* and *conventional pricing* rules such as "full cost" and "mark-up" pricing. While such price policies maximize profits only accidentally, they normally yield some economic profits, while protecting firms from the hazards of uncoordinated actions.

d. Oligopolistic prices are typically more stable than competitive prices. Price reductions tend to be strongly resisted, for fear of "spoiling the market" and setting off price wars. Price inflexibility is greater in downward direction than upward. In the face of buoyant demand or cost increases, price increases more easily occur, though usually at longer intervals than would be the case under competition.

e. The reluctance of oligopolistic firms to engage in price competition encourages the substitution of product competition as a means of enlarging market shares or maintaining given shares. *Product competition* takes the form of frequent changes in the differentiated products of each firm, and in extensive *advertising*.

f. From a social point of view, several objections to oligopolistic behavior can be raised. "Administered" instead of competitive pricing leads only accidentally to "correct" prices from a consumer point of view. When coordination of policies is effectively practiced, oligopoly approaches *monopoly*. The downward inflexibility of prices aggravates reductions in output and employment in periods of declining demand. The emphasis on product competition encourages costly changes of questionable utility and the assignment of scarce resources to the creation of advertising imagery.

On the positive side, in some industries oligopoly cannot be avoided without sacrificing *economies of scale*. This holds whenever minimum long-run average costs of production can be realized only when each firm's scale of output is so large that the market will support no more than a few firms. Additionally, the product competition of heterogeneous oligopoly increases product variety and enlarges the freedom of consumer choice. Finally, the large financial resources typically at the disposal of oligopolistic firms and their protected market positions may foster more extensive research and development than would occur under other market structures.

B CONCEPTS

1 Demand, Average Revenue, and Marginal Revenue

The *demand* for an individual firm's output shows the various quantities of its product that can be sold at various prices. The *demand curve* for the firm's product is identical with the firm's *average revenue curve*. If 100 units of product are demanded at a price of 10 cents and 120 units at a price of 9 cents, the firm's *revenue per unit of product* is 10 cents when 100 units are sold and 9 cents when 120 units are sold. For any volume of sales, *average revenue* is the same as the price of the product.

Average and marginal revenue are tied to each other by the *elasticity* of the demand or average revenue curve. (Mathematically, marginal revenue equals average revenue, or price, multiplied by one minus the reciprocal of the elasticity of the average revenue curve at that price.) If the average revenue curve is infinitely elastic (horizontal), marginal revenue is equal to average revenue. If the average revenue curve falls from left to right, marginal revenue is less than average revenue or price.

2   Optimum Output and Price

From a social point of view, the output and price of a product which best serve the interests of society are called the *optimum output and price.* Although there are certain exceptions, the general criteria for the optimum output and price consists of equal price and marginal costs.

3   Entry Conditions

Free entry into an industry means that new firms can be established without contrived barriers. *Restricted* entry supposes that certain barriers to entering an industry exist, but the possibility of doing so is not precluded. *Closed* entry means that for varied reasons new firms cannot be established in the industry.

4   Product Differentiation

The product of one firm is differentiated from that of other firms in the same industry if, in the minds of consumers, it is in some way different enough to that there is a basis for making a choice among them. The differences need not be real in a physical sense (though they may be), but simply the result of advertising, packaging, etc.

5   Selling Costs

Selling costs are connected with special efforts in the marketing of differentiated products. Fancy or unusual packaging, displays, and advertising are prime examples.

6   Price Wars

This term refers to the attempt of firms, usually in oligopolistic industries, to obtain a larger share of the market, and perhaps to drive other firms in the industry out of business by temporarily lowering prices. Other firms react by lowering their prices also, causing a chain reaction, until through the pressure of losses or as a result of agreement, the "war" is called off.

7   "Kinked" Demand Curve and Discontinuous Marginal Revenue Curve

A "kinked" demand curve contains a *corner*, as opposed to the normal smooth curve. The corner appears at the prevailing price of a firm's product.

Above that price the demand curve is less steeply sloped than it is below, as shown in Figure 16.1. At the corner, the elasticity of the curve changes sharply. Since marginal revenue is directly tied to the elasticity of demand, or average revenue, the marginal revenue curve has a discontinuous section at the prevailing price— that is, "jumps" from a higher to a lower level, like the *MR* curve in the figure.

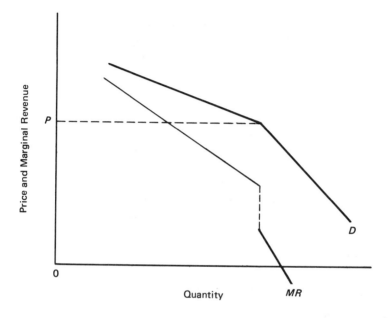

FIGURE 16.1 The "Kinked" Demand Curve

8 Price Leadership and Other Pricing Conventions

Price leadership is the practice, based on a tacit understanding among oligopolistic firm in an industry, of one firm setting a selling price, which other firms in the industry follow.

Full-cost pricing is simply the technique of setting price on the basis of average costs of production, plus a "reasonable" profit.

Mark-up pricing is similar, with price being determined by average costs, augmented by a conventional percentage mark-up.

9 Administered Prices

Administered prices are set by firms as a matter of discretionary choice, as opposed to competitive situations where price is outside the control of individual firms. The term is largely confined to oligopolistic markets and connotes price rigidity, especially in a downward direction.

C   DISCUSSION

1   Declining Average and Marginal Revenue

The demand and average revenue curve of a purely competitive firm is infinitely elastic at the prevailing market price, and thus identical with its marginal revenue curve. Demand is infinitely elastic because the firm can sell any amount it offers without affecting market price; it can sell nothing at any higher price—the consequence of the large number of firms in the industry and the negligible contribution of each one to total supply.

The demand and average revenue curve of an imperfectly competitive firm slopes downward (is less than infinitely elastic) because, given the demand curve for its product, it must lower the price to sell greater quantities of its product. Marginal revenue is therefore less than average revenue, or price, and also decreases with greater sales.

2   Monopoly Output and Price

A summary of the equilibrium output and price of a pure monopolist is shown graphically in Figure 16.2. The demand for the firm's output, equivalent to average revenue, is the curve labeled D. The associated marginal revenue curve is MR. AC and MC are the average and marginal cost curves.

Observe first that demand is elastic up to the quantity where the marginal revenue curve crosses the horizontal axis. At the point of intersection, marginal revenue is zero, indicating that the elasticity of demand for that quantity is *unity.* For greater sales, marginal revenue is *negative,* pointing up a corresponding area of *inelastic* demand. (See the expenditure test of elasticities in Chapter 12.)

The maximum profit output of the firm is O_q where marginal revenue and marginal costs are equal. The demand curve shows that sales of O_q command a price of OP.

The economic profits of the firm equal the difference between average revenue or price and average costs, ML, times the volume of output and sales, O_q or CM. This is equivalent to the area of the rectangle CPLM. Because of blocked entry into the industry, these profits may continue to be received without being eroded through competition.

Price under monopoly is necessarily higher than marginal costs, for marginal costs are equated with marginal revenue and marginal revenue must necessarily be less than price. However, the marginal utility of the good to consumers is measured by its price. (This is the result of rational consumer behavior, as described in Chapter 13.) Thus, the marginal utility of the good is higher than its marginal costs of production, indicating that output is below the socially desirable level.

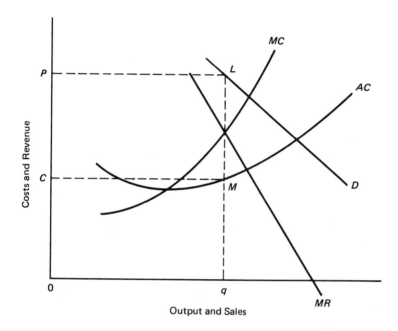

FIGURE 16.2 Monopoly Output and Price

Moreover, except by the accident of marginal revenue being equal to marginal costs at the lowest point on the average cost curve, monopoly output tends to be either less or greater than production at minimum average costs.

Because of these adverse social aspects, the formation of monopolies is opposed by federal antitrust laws. However, in some cases monopoly cannot be avoided, either because economies of scale would be seriously sacrificed if more than one firm is in the industry, or because the nature of the product requires one firm and one only to serve the public adequately (telephone service, for example). To capture the benefits in these cases of "natural" monopoly, while avoiding the worst abuses of monopoly power, the firms may be designated as public utilities, and their output and prices regulated by a public agency—such as a public utilities commission.

3 Output and Price Under Monopolistic Competition

Figure 16.3 shows the short- and long-run equilibrium positions of a firm under monopolistic competition.

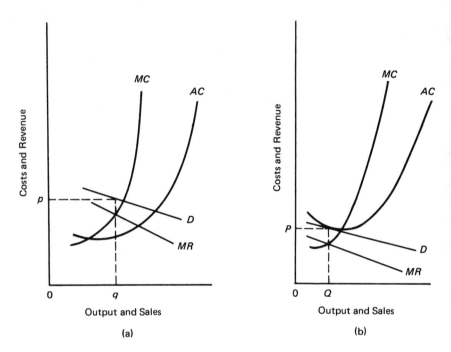

**FIGURE 16.3 Equilibrium Output and Price
of Monopolistically Competitive Firm**

In the short run, the maximum profit output is O_q, which sells at a price of O_p. Because this price is above average costs, the firm realizes economic profits. Since entry into the industry is free, the presence of economic profits induces new firms to come into the industry. This has the effect of pushing existing firms' demand curves downward and to the left. In long-run equilibrium, there are zero economic profits. This is shown in Figure 16.3(b) by the tangency of the firm's demand, or average revenue, curve with the average cost curve. Output is OQ and price OP, equal to average costs.

Note also, however, that even though economic profits are zero, the firm is maximizing its profits, for at output OQ marginal revenue equals marginal costs. (Because of the mathematical relationship between the elasticity of the average curve and the associated marginal value, at the output where the average revenue curve is tangent to the average cost curve, marginal revenue necessarily equals marginal costs.)

As in the case of monopoly, monopolistic competition price is always above marginal costs, while output tends to be produced at an average cost above the minimum. This shows that the industry's total output could be produced at lower costs, with fewer firms each producing a somewhat larger amount. In other words, excess capacity in this sense is characteristic of monopolistic competition. Moreover, costs are higher than under pure competition because of selling costs.

Monopolistic competition can be defended, however, as offering a greater variety of products to consumers. Also, competitive elements tend to force prices close to lowest average costs and to eliminate economic profits. And in any event, *pure* competition is not practical in many industries where products cannot be *standardized.*

4   Output and Price Under Oligopoly

a. The distinctive characteristic of oligopolistic market positions is the dependence of each firm's output and price decisions on the others in the industry. This interdependence results because each firm (or each of a few of the larger firms dominating the market) significantly affects the industry's market by its actions, with repercussions on the market position of other firms.

b. The uncertainty of an oligopolist about product demand arises out of this interdependence. How much sales will increase, if at all, as a result of lowering price depends upon the reaction of other firms: if other firms retain their prices, one firm could expect to increase its sales through a price reduction. But in self-defense other firms might also lower their prices, frustrating this attempt to obtain a larger share of the market. This also risks setting off a price war, from which the whole industry is likely to suffer.

The reaction to a single firm's raising price may be quite different. Other firms in the industry may be satisfied to keep their prices unchanged, since their market shares cannot shrink, but in fact are likely to increase through their products' lower cost. By the same token, the share of the firm raising its price will tend to decline, and it is this prospect which makes an independent price increase a risky move.

The combination of these possible reactions to an uncoordinated price change underlies the "kinked" demand curve and encourages some type of cooperation among oligopolistic firms, such as price leadership.

c. If price competition tends to be avoided in oligopoly, product competition is encouraged in heterogeneous oligopoly in the form of frequent style and model changes, extensive advertising, etc., since the risks of adverse repercussion are not the same as for price changes. Moreover, *all* industry firms usually engage in continued product changes, so that any firm failing to do so might find its sales and profits lagging.

d. There are both negative and positive social aspects in oligopoly. The antisocial tendency toward monopolistic restrictions of output motivates the public policy of watchfulness. The downward inflexibility of prices reduces the ability of the price system to absorb disturbances without reduced output and employment. For example, in a competitive market a shrinkage in demand is partly absorbed by a decrease in price; to the extent that price is maintained under oligopoly, the brunt of the impact falls on output. Excessive product differentiation (including "planned obsolescence") and advertising impose costs which many observers find difficult to justify.

On the other hand, oligopoly can hardly be avoided in such industries as automobiles; only the less acceptable monopoly market structure could be considered an alternative since the competitiveness of neither pure competition nor monopolistic competition is feasible; each of a large number of automobile firms would have to produce a small output at the sacrifice of significant economies of scale. If, for example, an output per firm of 500 thousand automobiles a year is required to realize fully the economies of scale, total annual sales of, say, 8 million cars would support a maximum of 16 firms—many more than now in the industry, but still far from a competitive market.

Finally, as to the greater variety of choice and the alleged advantage of oligopoly in fostering research and development—it is partly a matter of personal judgment and partly unsettled. No one can objectively say whether having new styles of automobiles each year is worth the cost. Nor is it perfectly clear that technological advances occur at a more rapid pace because of oligopoly, since much, if not most, of the basic research underlying such advances is carried on in universities and government-sponsored institutes. Moreover, there is evidence that some oligopolistic firms have suppressed technological changes to protect their investments in existing techniques.

D CONFUSIONS TO AVOID

1 The Meaning of Competition

In popular discussions frequent reference is made to the intense "competition" among oligopolistic firms. In its technical economic meaning, this is a misuse of the term since, in economic language, *competition* refers to a state in which the individual firm has no control over the price of its product, price being determined by impersonal forces in the marketplace. This is true only in what we have called purely competitive markets. It is least true in pure monopoly. In between these two poles, monopolistic competition falls closer to the competitive end of the spectrum and oligopoly closer to the monopolistic end.

2 Maximum-Profit Price

If a firm has control over the price of its product—as in pure monopoly, and to a lesser extent in coordinated oligopoly—it is sometimes thought that the firm will seek to set the highest possible price in order to maximize its profits. This is incorrect, for although a high price yields large revenue per unit of product sold, it restricts the number of units that can be sold: profits are the difference between total revenue and total costs. This difference is maximized by equating marginal revenue and marginal costs. A monopolistic firm usually charges a higher price than possible under competition because in following the maximum-profit rule it restricts output below the competitive level. No firm, including a monopolist, can ultimately control the demand for its product, though it is free to influence demand through advertising, etc.

CHAPTER 17 THE COMPETITIVE PRICING OF FACTOR SERVICES

A PRINCIPLES

1 Supply and Demand

In purely competitive markets, the price of the services of a productive resource (factor of production), like the price of a commodity, is subject to the law of *Supply and Demand*: the price of a factor service tends to the level where the quantity of the service demanded is equal to the quantity supplied.

2 Demand for a Factor Service

The demand for a factor service is derived from the demand for the goods which the factor helps to produce, and is equivalent to the marginal revenue product of the factor. Under pure competition, marginal revenue product is identical with the value of the marginal product of the factor.

3 Shape of the Demand Curve

Given the state of technology and constant amounts of other factor services, the marginal revenue product and value of the marginal product of a factor *decrease* as the quantity of the factor employed *increases*. More generally, an increase in the proportion in which a factor is combined with other factors tends to cause the marginal revenue product and value of the marginal product of the factor to decline. Hence, the demand curve for a factor service falls from left to right when the price of the service (W) is measured vertically and the quantity of the factor employed (Q) is measured horizontally, as in Figure 17.1.

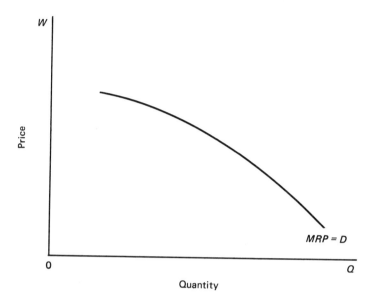

FIGURE 17.1   The Demand for a Factor Service

4   Elasticity of Demand

The *elasticity of demand* for a factor service is determined mainly by the substitutability of the factor for other factors in the production process, the importance of the service's cost in total costs, and the elasticity of demand for the good which the factor helps to produce.

a. The greater the substitutability of a factor, the greater the elasticity of demand for its services.

b. The more a factor service's cost contributes to total costs, the greater the elasticity of demand for it.

c. The more elastic the demand for the final output, the greater the elasticity of demand for a factor service.

5 Change in Demand

In constructing the demand for a factor service, all variables other than the price and quantity of the service are assumed to remain unchanged. In particular, the *demand* for the final product, the *quantity* and *prices* of other factor services, and the state of technology are assumed to remain constant.

A *change* in final output demand, or in the quantity or prices of other factor services, or in the state of technology, causes the demand for a factor service to change.

6 Factor Supply

The supplies of factor services vary according to the particular factor involved.

a. The supply of *land—i.e.,* nature-given resources—is *fixed* in the aggregate, with a price-elasticity of zero. For any factor service in zero elastic supply, price is determined by demand, with the return to the factor called an *economic rent.*

Particular pieces of land, with more than one use have an elasticity of supply greater than zero.

b. The aggregate supply of *labor* is based largely on noneconomic forces, such as population growth, age composition, prevailing practices with respect to labor force participation, the length of the work year, etc.

The supply of a particular kind of labor is determined by such things as the attractiveness or disutility of the work, the cost of training, and alternative opportunities.

While the supply curves of most types of labor have a positive price-elasticity over some range in wage rates, in some instances the curves have a *negative* elasticity (bend backward) above a certain wage level.

c. The supply of *capital* at any given time is the result of accumulated past *saving* and *investment* of society. Capital supply is diminished from use in current production; it is added to through current saving and investment.

B CONCEPTS

1 Supply and Demand of Factor Services

The same meaning is applied to demand and supply in connection with factor services as in connection with finished goods and services (see Chapter 12). In brief, demand and supply are each schedules relating quantities demanded and supplied to unit prices.

2 Marginal Revenue Product and Value of the Marginal Product

The *marginal revenue product* (*MRP*) of a factor is the addition to a firm's total revenue from a sale of the *extra* output for which an additional unit of factor input is responsible.

The additional output resulting from adding an extra unit of a factor input is the factor's *marginal physical product* (*MPP*) described in Chapter 15. The additional revenue resulting from selling an extra unit of output is the marginal revenue (*MR*). Hence, *marginal revenue product* (*MRP*) equals marginal physical product times marginal revenue:

$$MRP = MPP \times MR$$

The *value of the marginal product* (*VMP*) of a factor is simply the market value of the factor's marginal physical product. It is therefore equal to the marginal physical product times the market price (*P*) of the product:

$$VMP = MPP \times P$$

When marginal revenue is the same as price of the product, as under pure competition, *MRP* = *VMP*.

3 Elasticity of Factor Service Demand and Supply

As in the case of the price-elasticity of demand and supply for a final good (see Chapter 11), the elasticity of demand and supply of a factor service is equal to the ratio of the percentage change in the *quantity* demanded, or supplied, to the percentage change in the price of the factor service. Zero elasticity is represented by a vertical curve, infinite elasticity by a horizontal curve.

4 Economic Rent

In common usage, *rent* refers to the price of the services of land and plant and equipment. *Economic rent* which is in the nature of a surplus return to a factor, has the much broader sense of a payment that is not necessary in order for the factor's services to be supplied. The return to any factor that is fixed in supply—available for productive use whatever its price—is economic rent. If the price of a productive service is the least amount necessary to induce the service to be supplied, there is no economic rent present.

5 Classification of Factors

Labor, land, and capital are the three generic factors of production usually distinguished in economics. (A fourth factor, "entrepreneurship," is sometimes separately identified as a special subclass of labor.)

Labor embraces all human productive effort. *Land* includes all nature-given resources, in their original state. *Capital* consists of man-created instruments of production.

C DISCUSSION

1 Application of the Law of Supply and Demand

In a competitive market system, the prices commanded by productive services are determined in the same manner as the prices of final goods and services—*i.e.,* through the interaction of supply and demand.

If at a given price, the quantity of a particular factor service demanded exceeds (or falls short of) the quantity supplied, the price will be bid upward (or downward) until the quantities demanded and supplied are equal.

2 Demand for a Factor Service

The demand for factor services originates with the demand for output, since the only reason for hiring such services is for their contribution to the output of employing agencies.

A firm maximizes its profits by employing each factor service up to the point where the factor's marginal revenue product equals the price of the service. Profits are the difference between total revenue and total costs. Marginal revenue product is the addition to total revenue upon employing an extra unit of factor service. The price of the service, in competitive factor markets, measures the addition to the firm's costs of hiring an extra unit of the service. If extra revenue is larger (or smaller) than extra costs, profits can be increased by employing more (or fewer) units of the service until extra revenue and extra costs are equal.

This maximum-profit rule is equivalent from an input point of view to the maximum-profit rule of equating marginal costs and marginal revenue from an output point of view. The relationship between the two rules is as follows:

$$MC = \frac{W_i}{MPP_i}$$

$$MR = \frac{MRP_i}{MPP_i}$$

Hence, if $MC = MR$,

$$W_i = MRP_i$$

where MC is marginal costs, W_i is the price of the ith factor service, MPP_i is the marginal physical product of the ith factor, MRP_i is the marginal revenue product of the ith factor, and MR is the marginal revenue of the firm.

3 Shape of the Demand Curve for a Factor Service

Since the marginal revenue product of a factor is equivalent to the firm's demand curve for that factor's services, the demand curve assumes the same shape as the marginal revenue product curve.

Given the assumptions upon which a marginal revenue product curve is constructed—namely, given demand for final output, quantities and prices of other inputs, and state of technology—the curve falls from left to right. The marginal revenue product of a factor decreases as more of the factor is employed because the marginal physical product of the factor declines as a result of diminishing returns (law of Variable Proportions). Since the marginal revenue product is the product of marginal physical product and marginal revenue, a decrease in marginal physical product necessarily reduces marginal revenue product.

Another reason for the downward slope of the marginal revenue product curve is that in *imperfectly competitive* markets, marginal revenue also declines as output rises.

4 Elasticity of Demand for a Factor Service

The elasticity of demand for a factor service varies directly with the degree of substitutability between it and other factor services. If, for example, capital (such as certain types of machinery) can easily replace labor, and vice-versa, an increase in wage rates encourages the substitution of capital for labor, causing a relatively large decrease in the quantity of labor demanded.

Elasticity of demand for a factor service also varies directly with the importance of its costs as part of the total costs of the firm. If wage costs are 75 percent of total factor costs, an increase in wage rates results in a greater rise in total costs than if wages were only 50 percent of total costs. Consequently, the response in the quantity of labor demanded to a wage rate rise would be greater in the first case.

The role of the elasticity of demand for the final products in determining the elasticity of demand for input services is based on the *derived* nature of the demand for factor services. If final product demand is elastic, a higher product price—because of a higher factor service price—results in a relatively large contraction in the quantity of product demanded, hence in factor service demanded.

5 Changes in Demand for Factor Services

The demand (*i.e.,* the whole schedule or curve) for a factor service rises or falls with increases or decreases in the demand for the products which the factor helps to produce. If the demand for bread increases, the demand for the land, labor, and capital used to raise wheat increases.

The quantities and prices of other factor services affect the demand for a given factor service because of their influence on the productivity of the service and because of substitutability. The greater the quantity of land and capital with which labor works, the greater the marginal revenue product tends to be, and hence the demand for labor. The higher the prices of other factor services, the greater the demand for a given factor service to serve in place of the others. (NOTE: if factor services are complementary instead of substitutive, demand for a given service varies in the *opposite* direction as changes in the prices of other factor services.)

Finally, a technological change, by changing the productivity of a factor, shifts the demand for the factor's services in the same direction.

6 Economic Rent and the Elasticity of Supply of Factor Services

Economic rent is present in the price of a factor service whose elasticity of supply is less than infinite. In general, the elasticity of supply of a factor service will be less than infinite whenever there are alternative uses of the factor, or, in the case of produced capital goods, when there are increasing supply prices.

The price necessary to keep a factor from shifting to another use is called the "transfer price". The excess price of a factor service above its transfer price is *economic rent.*

7 The Supply of Labor

a. The total supply of labor depends upon the size of population, the portion of the population in the labor force, and the average number of hours worked.

Given the size of population (which is determined by numerous complex variables of noneconomic as well as economic character) and current attitudes toward working ages, the role of women, etc., the supply of labor is a function of wage rates.

Up to a point, a greater quantity of hours of labor is offered the higher the wage rate per hour, so that the supply curve of labor service displays the usual characteristic of sloping upward. However, at some relatively high wage rate, a maximum quantity of labor service is reached with the quantity actually decreasing beyond that wage rate. Over such a range in wage rates, the supply curve bends backward; that is, it becomes one of negative elasticity.

The explanation of the strange shape of the supply curve of labor lies in the relative strength of two influences: the substitution effect and the income effect. Starting at the lower end of the wage scale, as the wage rate rises, workers may wish to substitute income for leisure—that is, to work longer hours. As the wage rate reaches and goes beyond some higher level, however, workers tend to "purchase" more leisure by working fewer hours. Over the upsloping section of the supply curve of labor service, the substitution effect becomes stronger than the income effect; the switch in their relative strength occurs as the curve bends backward.

b. The supply curves for particular types of labor or in particular occupations depend on several considerations. Labor of a given quality (skill, training, etc.) may be attracted to one occupation more strongly than to another because of differences in nonmonetary aspects of the work— the pleasantness of the work, safety factors, status attaching to the occupation, etc. In such cases the supply tends to be larger for the preferred work and, in the absence of differences in demand, the wage rate lower for that work. Differences in wage rates of this type are called *equalizing differences.*

Supply curves for different types of labor may, on the other hand, be the result of differences in skills and training and the costs of acquiring them. Skilled labor tends to be in shorter supply than more common types of labor and, consequently, wage rates tend to be higher. Over the long run, higher wage rates induce more workers to acquire the training and skills necessary to qualify for such work. In the short run, however, it is not possible to do this, so that large wage differentials among occupations exist. Such wage rate differentials are due to the immobility of workers among occupations; and the workers are said to be in noncompeting groups.

8 The Supply of Capital

Capital, consisting of manmade means of production, is accumulated through saving and net investment. *Saving* is the act of refraining from consuming entire income; *net investment* is expenditure on currently produced goods that are added to the stock of goods (rather than consumed or used to replace worn-out capital).

In the short run, the stock of accumulated capital from past saving and net investment is zero elastic—that is, graphically it appears as a vertical line.

9 The Supply of Land

Land, defined in the classical sense as nature-given means of production, is fixed in supply in the short run, although in the long run its quality (and even its quantity) can be changed through the application of labor and capital and as the result of exploitation. Looked at from the point of view of the economy as a whole, land rent is the prototype of economic rent because land has virtually a zero elasticity of supply. However, the elasticity of supply of a particular parcel of land is greater than zero whenever it has alternative uses—as is nearly always the case. If a tract can be used either to raise wheat or corn, its supply price for one use cannot be less than that for the other. To enlarge the quantity of land supplied, say, for wheat, the rental price is bid up to attract it away from corn growing.

D CONFUSIONS TO AVOID

1 Factor Service Prices and Factor Prices

Throughout this discussion the prices of the services of productive factors, not of the factors themselves, have been discussed. In a market economy, except for labor, the factors of production as well as their services are bought and sold and so command market prices. Land may be bought—or the services of land rented. A building or other capital good can be bought—or its services bought. From an economic point of view, it makes no difference in the long run whether a firm owns the land and capital it uses, or whether it hires these services from other owners.

The value (price) of productive factors is directly related to the market prices their services command. The process of calculating the value of a factor on the basis of the price of its productive services is called capitalization, and is briefly described in Section E following.

2 The Relationship Between Output and Input Approaches

The production process consists of appropriately combining inputs to achieve the desired outputs. Inputs are the services of various factor resources— land, labor, capital. The technical relationship between inputs and output is given by the production function, described in Chapter 15.

From an overall, or general equilibrium point of view, the pricing of inputs and outputs, being parts of a single process, cannot be separated. The price of an output depends upon costs of production; costs of production depend upon the prices of factor services; the prices of factor services depend upon the prices of outputs.

However, it is convenient, especially for expository purposes, to concentrate each aspect separately—this is partial equilibrium analysis. Concentrating on the output side, our primary interest is final product prices. For this purpose, assuming that input prices are given, we seek the determinants of a firm's output and pricing decisions, applying the maximum-profit rule of equating marginal revenue and marginal costs. Concentrating on the input side, our primary interest is in factor service pricing and costs of production. For this purpose, final product prices are taken as given, and the rule of equating marginal revenue product and the price of each factor service is applicable.

E CAPITALIZATION

1 The Pricing of Factor Resources

The value of a factor resource is found by *capitalizing* its yield, determining the present value of a future stream of income.

Suppose that an asset has a rental price of $100 per year which is expected to continue indefinitely into the future. The question then is what this perpetual $100 per year income is worth at the moment. The question can be put in reverse: how much would have to be invested now in order to receive a perpetual annual income of $100? The answer is given by the prevailing rate of interest. If the rate of interest on loan funds is 5 percent, a $2,000 loan would yield $100 per year. Thus, a perpetual annual income of $100 is worth $2,000 today, if the rate of interest is 5 percent. If the rate of interest were different, so too would be the present value of a future income stream: at a rate of 10 percent, an annual income flow of $100 is worth only $1,000 today.

The general relationship between the present value of an asset (PV) and its perpetual annual yield (A) is given by the following formula (where i is the rate of interest):

$$PV = \frac{A}{i}$$

It is clear from the formula that the present value of an asset varies inversely with the rate of interest. When the market rate of interest changes, the value of income-yielding assets changes in the opposite direction.

CHAPTER 18   FACTOR SERVICE PRICING IN IMPERFECTLY COMPETITIVE MARKETS

A   PRINCIPLES

1   Forms of Imperfect Competition in Factor Pricing

Imperfect competition in factor service pricing occurs as the result of any one of four market situations:

> imperfect competition in *product* markets
> imperfect competition on the buyers' side of factor service markets—*monopsony*
> imperfect competition on the sellers' side of factor service markets—*monopoly*, or
> a combination of the last two—*bilateral monopoly.*

2   Imperfectly Competitive Product Markets

Imperfectly competitive product markets restrict the demand for factor services below competitive levels. Both the prices of factor services and the quantities employed, other things being equal, are less under imperfect competition in product markets than under purely competitive product markets.

3   Monopsony

In *monopsonistic* factor service markets, demand is also restricted, as compared to competitive factor service markets, with both factor service prices and quantities employed falling below competitive levels.

4 Factor Monopoly

In *monopolistic* factor service markets, supply is restricted below competitive levels, causing above-competitive factor service prices but below-competitive employment.

5 Bilateral Monopoly

In *bilateral monopoly,* factor service employment is restricted below competitive levels, but factor service prices are indeterminant within an upper and lower range.

B CONCEPTS

1 Imperfect Product Markets

Imperfect competition in product markets refers to the presence of monopoly, monopolistic competition, or oligopoly, as discussed in Chapter 16.

2 Monopsony

Monopsony refers to monopoly in *buying,* as opposed to selling. In "pure" monopsony, there is only one buyer. More usually there is more than one buyer of a factor service, but when there are so few buyers that each one influences the market price of the service by his actions, some degree of monopsony is present.

3 Monopolistic Factor Markets

Monopolistic factor service markets exist when the sellers of factor services are able to influence factor service prices by controlling *supply.* Pure monopoly means there is only one seller of a factor service without close substitutes.

4 Bilateral Monopoly

Bilateral monopoly is a combination of monopsony and monopoly in factor markets. The chief example relates to union-management negotiations when the workers in an industry are represented by union officials, and the industry is represented by chosen spokesmen.

C DISCUSSION

1 Demand for Factor Services Under Imperfect Competition

Imperfectly competitive product markets affect factor service demand since the latter is *derived* from final product demand.

More specifically, the demand for a factor service—equivalent to the marginal revenue product (*MRP*) curve of the factor—is *below* the competitive level.

Marginal revenue product (*MRP*) equals marginal physical product (*MPP*) of the factor, times marginal revenue (*MR*) from the sale of output:

$$MRP = MPP \times MR$$

Under pure competition, marginal revenue equals price of the product (*P*), so that $MRP = MPP \times P$. Under imperfect competition, marginal revenue is *less* than the price of the product: $MR < P$. Hence, the *MRP* is less under imperfect competition than under pure competition. Stated differently, under pure competition marginal revenue product is the same as the *value of the marginal product* (*VMP*), while under imperfect competition $MRP < VMP$. In Figure 18.1, *D*, equal to *VMP*, is the competitive firm's demand curve for a factor service, while *D'*, equal to *MRP*, would be the imperfectly competitive firm's demand curve. With supply of the factor service indicated by *S*, the effect of imperfect competition is to lower employment of the service from *q* to *q'* and its price from *w* to *w'*.

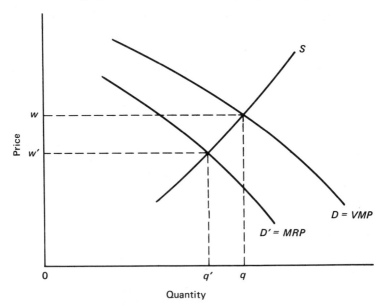

FIGURE 18.1 Demand for Factor Service in Imperfect Competition

2 Supply of Factor Services Under Monopsony

In purely competitive factor markets, the supply of a factor service to the individual firm is infinitely elastic (horizontal) at the prevailing market price of the service. Under monopsony, the supply curve of the factor service rises from left to right, since the firm must offer higher prices for the factor service to purchase greater quantities of it. In this case, the firm does not maximize profits by equating the *MRP* of the factor with its price, but rather through equating *MRP* with the marginal resource cost (*MRC*) of the factor.

The *MRC* is the addition to the firm's factor service cost resulting from employing an extra unit of the factor service. For example, suppose that ten units of labor can be hired at a wage of $10 per day per worker, but that to hire eleven units a wage of $10.50 is necessary. The extra cost to the firm of employing the eleventh unit of labor is then $15.50 (the difference in total wage costs between $10 \times \$10 =$

To maximize profits, the firm must equate the additional revenue realized from hiring an extra unit of factor service (the *MRP* of the factor) and the additional cost imposed (the *MRC*).

If the supply curve of a factor service rises from left to right, the marginal resource cost of the service lies above the supply curve, as illustrated in Figure 18.2. The firm's maximum profit employment of the factor is O_q. The price paid the service is Ow, which is wm less than the factor's marginal revenue product.

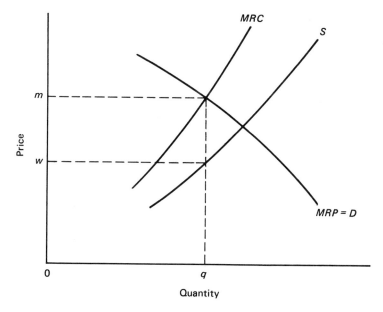

FIGURE 18.2 Monopsonistic Resource Demand

3   Bilateral Monopoly

If a factor service is monopolistically supplied *and* demanded—a bilateral monopoly situation—the price of the service will fall somewhere between the minimum price the supplier is willing to accept and the maximum the buyer will pay. The minimum acceptable supply price may be determined arbitrarily by the monopolistic seller, but the price presumably would be set above the competitive level. The maximum acceptable demand price is equal to the level at which the marginal resource cost of the service is equal to the marginal revenue product of the service.

Where the price will actually be within this range depends upon the relative bargaining strength of the two parties, their skills as negotiators, their relative "holding" power (such as labor union strike funds and the financial position of the firms involved), etc.

D   CONFUSIONS TO AVOID

1   Interrelationship of Product and Factor Markets

Remember that product markets and factor service markets are interrelated. Imperfectly competitive product markets will reflect back on factor service markets, and vice-versa.

Note that there are four possible combinations of product-factor service market structures:

> pure competition in both markets,
> pure competition in product markets, imperfect competition in factor markets,
> pure competition in factor markets, imperfect competition in product markets, and
> imperfect competition in both markets.

In general, imperfect competition in product markets restricts the demand for factor services, as compared to pure competition, Monopsonistic markets also restrict factor service demand, while monopoly in selling factor services tends to cut down factor service supply. All these cases, and the various combinations, cause factor service prices and employment to deviate from competitive levels.

CHAPTER 19 THE MARKET DISTRIBUTION OF INCOME

A PRINCIPLES

1 Marginal Productivity and Functional Distribution

With competitive product and factor service markets, the division of national income into factor shares—the *functional distribution of income*—is determined by the *marginal productivity* of the factors, in conjunction with supplies, each factor receiving a return equal to the value of its marginal product.

2 Determinants of Marginal Productivity

The marginal productivity of a factor is determined by:

a. The *quantity* of the factor employed, relative to the quantities of other factors employed—the smaller the relative quantity of a factor, the greater its marginal productivity.

b. The productive *quality* of the factor—*e.g.*, the level of skills possessed by labor. Higher quality is associated with higher productivity.

c. The productive qualities of other, cooperating factors—*e.g.*, the better the quality of land and capital with which labor works, the greater the marginal productivity of the labor (as well as of the other factors).

d. The demand for the final products which the factor's services help produce. This is especially important when the services of a particular factor are heavily used in producing particular products.

e. The present state of technology.

3   Effect of Imperfect Competition

In imperfectly competitive product and/or factor markets, a factor tends to receive less than the value of its marginal product.

4   Personal Distribution

The *personal distribution* of income depends upon the combination of the market pricing of factor services (the functional distribution of income) and the distribution of ownership of factors. The latter is determined largely by noneconomic forces of historical, social, and political character.

B   CONCEPTS

1   Functional and Personal Income Distribution

Functional distribution refers to the division of income according to the type of productive resources responsible for the income. The two broadest types of productive factors are human and nonhuman, or labor and capital (or property). The corresponding functional shares are wages, on the one hand, and interest, rents, and profits on the other. Conceptually, the latter category can be broken down into its component parts, though in practice it is difficult to do so.

The *personal* distribution of income refers not to the factor origins of the income, but rather to the individual and family recipients. The usual measurement of personal distribution is in terms of class-size of income, such as the number of individuals and families receiving under $2,000 per year, the number receiving between $2,000 and $4,000 per year, etc. When the number in each class-size and the total income received by each class are expressed in percentages of the total number of individuals and families and of total personal income, respectively, a measure of the degree of inequality in distribution is yielded. A perfectly equal distribution would exist if the different percentages of the population received equivalent percentages of total income.

2   Marginal Product

The marginal product of a factor is the addition to the total product resulting from the employment of an extra factor unit—with the quantities of other, cooperating factors held constant. The *value* of the marginal product is found by multiplying the marginal (physical) product by the price per unit of the product.

3 Technology

Technology refers to the application of knowledge to production processes. The state of technology at any given time therefore depends on current knowledge about technical input-output relationships, and the extent to which this can feasibly be put to practical use in current productive activity.

4 The Distribution of Factor Ownership

An individual's market income is equal to the amount of productive services he provides multiplied by the market prices of these services. For those who own no productive resources other than their own labor, wages are the sole source of market income. For those who own productive property (capital, land), income is received in the form of interest, rentals, or profits instead of, or in addition to, wages. How the ownership of income-yielding property is distributed has an effect on how income is distributed.

C DISCUSSION

1 Functional Distribution in Pure Competition

In purely competitive markets, the price of each factor service is equal to the value of its marginal product. This is the result of each firm's efforts to maximize its profits. As seen before (see Chapter 17), to maximize profits a firm must equate the marginal revenue product (in pure competition equal to the value of the marginal product) of each factor to the marginal resource cost of the factor (in pure competition equal to the price of the factor's service). Hence, in equilibrium the price of each factor service equals the value of its marginal product in all its uses.

2 Determinants of Marginal Productivity

a. The marginal productivity of a factor varies inversely with its *relative quantity* because of the law of Diminishing Returns, or Variable Proportions.

b. The higher the quality a factor possesses, the greater its marginal productivity: a skilled worker has a higher productivity than an unskilled worker.

c. The quality of cooperating factors affects the productivity of a factor, since output is the joint product of all the factors engaged. Good entrepreneurship, or management, makes for greater productivity of each engaged factor than would be the case with inefficient management.

d. The value of marginal products depends upon both the physical productivity of the factors and the prices of their output. If demand for a particular product is low, resulting in a low market value, the value of a given marginal product will also be low. Hence, any factor with no or limited alternatives would command a low price for its services.

e. Marginal productivity depends in part on the state of technology. If improved methods of production are introduced as a result of new knowledge or the application of existing knowledge, the productivity of some, or all, factors increases.

3 Effect of Imperfect Competition

In imperfectly competitive markets, factor prices are less than under pure competition because demand for factor services is smaller. Demand is smaller either because marginal revenue products are less than the values of marginal products (when firms sell their products in imperfectly competitive markets), or because firms restrict their purchase of inputs under rising marginal resource costs (under monopsonistic factor markets).

4 Personal Distribution

How the national income is divided among individuals and families depends, given the functional distribution, upon the distribution of factor ownership. An individual may have a low income either because he possesses a small quantity of factor resources, or because the market prices of the factors he owns are low.

The ownership of property—land and capital—is usually unequally distributed, thereby contributing to the unequal distribution of personal income. However, even if property were equally distributed, there would still tend to be considerable inequality in personal incomes because of the differences in market wage rates for different kinds of labor services.

D   CONFUSIONS TO AVOID

1   Ethics versus Explanation

The principles behind the market distribution of income contain no *ethical,* or *normative,* implications. The statement that under pure competition a person will tend to receive an income equal to the market value of his (and his property's) marginal contribution to the economy's output is an explanation of principles, not a justification of them. What is regarded as a "fair" or "just" distribution of income is an ethical or political judgment falling outside the province of economics.

PART V
PUBLIC FINANCE

CHAPTER **20** PUBLIC FINANCE

A PRINCIPLES

1 Roles of Government Expenditure and Taxes

The amount and kinds of government expenditure and taxes affect the *level, composition,* and *distribution* of the national income.

2 Level of National Income

Goverment expenditure on goods and services is an *injection* into the income-expenditure stream; taxes are a *leakage* from the stream: other things being equal, the greater the government expenditure, the higher the national income; the greater the taxes, the lower the national income.

3 Composition of National Income

a. The allocation of resources between public and private goods and services is measured by the proportion of the national income accounted for by government expenditure. In periods of full employment, government expenditure diverts resources from the *private* sectors.

b. Taxes serve the allocative function of shifting resources from the production of private goods and services to the provision of *public* goods and services.

158

4   Income Distribution

    a. Government expenditure affects the distribution of real income to the extent that public goods and services are not consumed in amounts proportional to the incomes of the consumers.

    b. Taxes (including transfer payments as *negative* taxes) affect the distribution of income to the extent that tax payments are not proportional to the incomes of taxpayers. Proportional taxes do not affect the personal distribution of income; progressive taxes redistribute income in the direction of greater equality; regressive taxes redistribute income in the direction of less equality.

    Certain taxes may be shifted from those who immediately pay them to others upon whom the *incidence* of the taxes falls. The shiftability of taxes is greater when the demand and supply of the affected goods are *less elastic.*

5   Principles of Government Expenditure

    The allocation of resources to the government sector may be justified on distributional grounds, because of the public nature of certain goods and services, external (or third-party) effects, or economies of scale.

6   Principles of Taxation

    The two leading principles of taxation are the *benefits* and *ability-to-pay* principles.

B   CONCEPTS

1   Types of Taxes

    A *progressive* tax takes a higher proportion of a taxpayer's income, the higher his income is. It is best illustrated by the federal individual income tax.

    A *regressive* tax takes a lower proportion of a taxpayer's income, the higher his income is. A sales tax on a necessity or widely consumed good is a good example.

    A *proportional* tax takes the same proportion of the income of all taxpayers. A flat (constant-rate) state or municipal income tax is the best example.

2   Incidence and Shifting of Taxes

The *incidence* of a tax is the final resting place of the burden of the tax. If a tax is shifted, those who pay the tax are not the ones who ultimately bear its cost.

3   Public Goods

A *public good* is one whose consumption by one individual does not affect its consumption by others. Individuals cannot be excluded from consuming the good if it is provided at all. Such public services as national defense, flood control, control of water and air pollution, are examples.

4   External Effects

External effects are the costs or benefits imposed upon (or received by) the *community* which are not reflected in the costs or price of the producing unit. The discharge of factory waste material into a stream or the air imposes costs on the community in the form of higher medical bills, greater cleaning or purification expenses, etc.

External or third-party benefits are well illustrated by educational services. Not only do the individuals receiving these services gain, but so too does society.

5   Benefit and Ability-to-Pay Principles of Taxation

The *benefit* principle is that taxes should be paid in accordance with the benefits received by the taxpayer. The *ability-to-pay* principle is that different taxpayers should bear the burden of taxes according to their ability, usually measured by income.

C   DISCUSSION

1   Level of National Income

See Chapter 7 for the explanation of the role of government expenditure and taxation in determining the level of the national income.

2   Composition of Income

When there is full employment, the allocation of resources for one use prevents other, alternative uses of these resources. (This is not true when there are unemployed resources which can be drawn upon without affecting existing production; in this case the role of *countercyclical fiscal policy* becomes important). The greater the provision of goods and services by government during periods of full employment, the less available are private goods and services.

The basic function of taxes is to release resources from the production of private goods and services for use in producing the goods and services furnished by government. This is accomplished because taxes reduce disposable private income, and thereby demand for private goods and services.

3   Income Distribution

Government expenditure affects income distribution because, although government-provided goods and services are *part* of the national income, they are not distributed among individuals according to income. Although most public goods and services are equally available to everyone, in most cases they are not equally consumed. Probably the bias is in the direction of greater consumption, in proportion to income, by lower-income groups; therefore the distributive effect of government expenditure is toward greater equality.

Progressive taxes also work in the direction of greater real income equality. This clearly would be the case if the tax proceeds were distributed in cash in inverse proportion to income, or even equally, among the population. Essentially the same effect is produced by the distribution of public goods and services.

Regressive taxes work in the opposite direction, toward greater inequality in income. With the proportion of income paid in taxes rising as income falls, lower-income groups are left with a smaller share of the real national income.

Only *proportional* taxes leave the personal distribution of income unaffected. If everyone pays, say, 10 percent of his income, each one's share of national income is the same as before the tax.

Care must be exercised in determining who ultimately pays a tax, because the *incidence* may be different from the initial point of levy. Most taxes are shiftable to some degree. In general, the shiftability of taxes varies directly with the inelasticity of the demand and supply curves of the good or service being taxed.

For example, a tax on the production of a good (such as a manufacturing excise tax) reduces the competitive supply curve by the amount of the tax. Graphically, this is shown by a vertical displacement *upward* of the supply curve, as in Figure 20.1 from SS to $S'S'$.

With demand DD, the price of the good rises from P to P' as a result of the tax of TP'. Part of the tax is thus shifted from the producers to the purchasers of the good. If the demand were less elastic, the rise in price would be greater and a greater part of the tax shifted to purchasers.

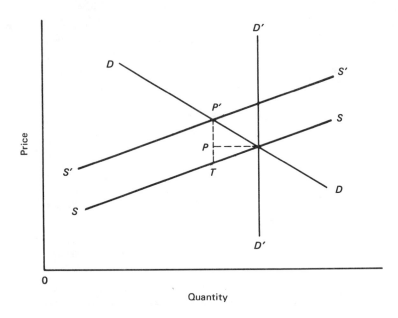

FIGURE 20.1 The Shifting of a Tax

In the extreme case of a *zero elastic* demand, such as $D'D'$ in Figure 20.1, the price rises by the full amount of the tax, with complete forward shifting.

Taxes on production and sales usually are partially shifted to purchasers. They are *regressive* in their income effects; their regressivity arises when a larger fraction of income of the lower-income groups than of higher-income groups is spent on the taxed goods. Consequently, the tax paid as a percentage of income is higher for the lower-income taxpayer. Property taxes, which are the primary source of revenue for local government, tend to be regressive.

4 Principles of Government Expenditure

Some government expenditure is based directly on distributional objectives. Such is the case, for example, in low-income housing projects and the distribution of surplus food. The largest portion of government expenditure, however, is based on other considerations, even though the distribution of income is affected.

The least controversial principle underlying government expenditure is that of providing goods and services that private markets are incapable of supplying satisfactorily. *Public goods* are the clearest-cut case, since by their nature private production and distribution are not feasible. The appropriate level of output of such a good is, however, a subject of much dispute, settled usually on political grounds.

Falling into a related category are certain goods the production or consumption of which has strong external effects. Many governmental goods and services are included here: streets and highways, bridges, police and fire protection, health and sanitation services, and education are prime examples.

Finally, economies of scale may justify the public provision of certain goods or services as an alternative to the regulation of their private production. For example, a municipality may produce and distribute electricity, gas, and water for this reason.

5   Principles of Taxation

The benefit principle of taxation is founded on the concept that one should get what he pays for, as in market transactions. Even if the ethics of the principle are accepted, however, it is not an operational basis for most government expenditures because of the difficulties in separating and measuring benefits. The benefits of public goods are more or less diffused over the entire community, and when there are important external effects, there is no practical way of identifying the particular third parties who benefit, or of assessing the values of the benefits.

The ability-to-pay principle is founded mainly on the ethical premise that it is "fair" and "just" for tax burdens to fall more heavily on higher than on lower income groups. It can be argued, though not conclusively proved, that taxes amounting to, say, 25 percent of a $10,000 income are no more burdensome than a 10 percent tax on a $5,000 income.

Certain taxes are specifically designed to redistribute market income toward greater equality. The federal personal income tax, and gift and estate taxes are the chief examples.

D   CONFUSIONS TO AVOID

1   The Various Functions of Taxes

Taxes play multiple roles in the economy. They affect *aggregate expenditure,* and thus the level of production, income, and employment. They affect the *allocation of resources* between the private and public sectors. (Taxes also introduce a distortion in the price mechanism which guides resource allocation in a market system. This allocation aspect has been ignored in the present discussion.) They also affect the *distribution of income.*

Even though in actuality these different effects are intermixed, they should be kept clearly separated in analytical thinking. The separation is important in policy formation, since in seeking to serve one kind of goal through a tax measure, other goals may be compromised.

2 Public Goods

In a general, popular sense, public goods are any goods and services furnished by government instead of in the market place. In its technical economic meaning, a *public good* is one which, because of its nature, cannot feasibly be produced and distributed through market channels. Thus, while postal services, for example, are a public good in the first sense, they are not in the technical sense.

PART VI

CHAPTER **21** INTERNATIONAL
ECONOMIC RELATIONS

A   PRINCIPLES

1   International Trade

International trade consists of the exchange of goods and services among countries. The goods and services sold to other countries are *exports*; the goods and services purchased from other countries are *imports.*

2   Law of Comparative Advantage

A country tends to produce and *export* goods and services in which it has a *comparative cost advantage* and to *import* those for which it has a *comparative cost disadvantage.* This is called the law of *Comparative Advantage.*

3   Bases of Comparative Advantage

A country has a comparative advantage in those goods and services produced with its most abundant and available factor resources and a comparative disadvantage in those goods and services produced with its relatively scarcest factor resources. More specifically, a country's comparative advantage lies in those goods and services whose production requires relatively large amounts of abundant factor resources.

4   Benefits of Trade

The real income of the world and the real national incomes of individual countries are increased by international trade based on comparative advantage. Social gain from trade arises from the efficiencies produced by exchange and specialization in production. Additional benefits conferred by trade include greater variety of consumer choice and more competitive market structures.

5   International Factor Movements

In addition to the international movement of goods and services, mobile *factors of production*—labor and capital—have an economic motive to migrate to countries where the real rates of return are higher. The emigration of labor proceeds from relatively labor-abundant countries to labor-scarce countries. Capital tends to move from capital-abundant countries to relatively capital-scarce countries.

6   Relationship Between Trade and Factor Movements

Trade and factor movements are explained by the same basic set of forces— the unequal relative national endowments of productive factors—and both have the same general effects on income. Trade and factor movements are therefore substitutes for each other.

7   Effects of Trade and Factor Movements on Income Distribution

Trade and factor movements affect not only the *level* of world and national income but also its *distribution* within each country; these tend to increase the absolute and relative income share of the more abundant factors and reduce the share of the scarcer factors.

8   Controls Over Trade and Factor Movements

Governments interfere with free trade and factor movements by interposing artificial barriers: import tariffs and quotas, immigration restrictions, and capital controls.

B   CONCEPTS

1   Comparative Advantage and Disadvantage

Comparative advantage can be distinguished from *absolute advantage:* if the cost of producing a good is cheaper in country *A* than in country *B*, as measured in some *common unit*, *A* has an *absolute* advantage in that good. *Comparative* costs, on the other hand, refer to the cost of one good relative to the cost of another good. As an example, consider two goods, *X* and *Y,* and two countries, *A* and *B,* with the following cost situation:

	A	B
X	$ 1	200 pesos
Y	$10	600 pesos

It is not possible with the information given to make *absolute* cost comparisons between the two countries, but *comparative* costs are readily calculable. In *A,* the cost of *Y* is ten times the cost of *X*; in *B*, the cost of *Y* is three times the cost of *X*. Hence, good *Y* is relatively more costly in country *A* than in country *B*. Necessarily, good *X* is therefore cheaper in *A* than in *B* (1/10 as expensive as *Y* in country *A* and 1/3 as expensive as *Y* in country *B*). Country *A* has a comparative cost *advantage* in good *X* and *disadvantage* in good *Y*; the opposite is true for country *B*.

2   Relative Factor Endowments

Relative factor endowments involve the comparison between countries of the quantities of their productive resources. As in the case of comparative costs, the comparison is not in absolute, but in relative, terms.

A country is said to be relatively labor-abundant and capital-scarce if the quantity of labor available to it, compared to the amount of the capital it possesses, is greater than the quantity of labor compared to capital possessed by other countries. Relative capital abundance involves labor scarcity, and vice versa.

3   Factor Movements

Factor movements refer to the relocation of the means of production from one country to another. *Land* cannot physically be moved—*i.e.,* it is perfectly immobile—but labor and capital are physically mobile and may be transferred among countries.

The movement of labor means the emigration and then immigration of those belonging to the labor force. The movement of capital refers not to capital goods (which are included in international trade), but to the movement of monetary and financial claims and evidences of debt or ownership, as recorded in the capital account of the balance of payments (see Chapter 11). In real terms, capital can move internationally only in the form of a net movement of goods and services. For example, if there is a capital movement of $100 million from country A to country B, the transfer takes place in the form of an export surplus in A and an import surplus in B, each of $100 million.

4   Tariffs and Quotas

A *tariff* is a tax levied on goods crossing national boundaries. Most tariffs are on goods entering the country (import tariffs), though tariffs may also be levied on goods leaving the country (export tariffs), or even on goods passing through the country (*transit* tariffs).

A *quota* is a quantitative limitation on a good entering (import quota) or leaving (export quota) a country. While any amount of a foreign good may be imported as long as a tariff is paid, in the case of an import quota, the good may be imported only until the quota is reached. (Quotas usually are specified for one-year periods and renewable in succeeding years.)

5   Terms of Trade

The terms of trade are the ratio at which a country's exports of goods and services are exchanged in world markets for its imports. An improvement in the terms of trade occur if export prices rise relative to import prices: a given volume of exports has been exchanged internationally for a larger volume of imports. If relative export and import prices move in the opposite direction, the terms of trade deteriorate and a given volume of exports commands in exchange a *smaller* volume of imports.

C   DISCUSSION

1   Law of Comparative Advantage

The operation of this principle can most easily be illustrated with a simple illustration of a pretrade cost situation for goods X and Y in countries A and B:

	A	B
X	$ 1	200 pesos
Y	$10	600 pesos

The law of comparative advantage as applied here states that country A will tend to specialize in and export good X and import good Y, with country B following the opposite course. This pattern of trade develops when each country can obtain the good it imports at a lower social economic cost than if the good were to be produced at home. This will be the case if country A can obtain one unit of good Y in exchange for the export of any amount of good X less than ten units; and if country B can obtain for one unit of good Y exported any amount more than three units of X. Clearly both these conditions are simultaneously fulfilled on any terms of trade falling between $1Y \leqslant 10X$ and $1Y \geqslant 3X$.

The limits to the possible terms at which trade will occur are set by the domestic cost ratios in the two countries: exactly where the terms of trade are established is determined by the requirements of the balance of payments. But let us assume in our example that terms of $1Y = 6X$ produce an equality in the values of each country's exports and imports. Country A, then, for six units of X exported obtains one unit of Y in return. For a unit of Y output obtained at home without trade, country A would have to sacrifice ten units of X output.

From country B's point of view, a similar advantage is gained: for each unit of Y exported, six units of X are obtained in exchange. But to produce six units of X at home without trade would require the sacrifice of two units of Y output.

Generalizing, we may say that, with the opportunity of trading present, goods and services tend to be produced in those regions and countries where it is relatively least costly. This is an application of the general economic principle of minimizing costs and maximizing output.

2 Factor Endowments and Comparative Advantage

A country tends to have a comparative advantage in those goods which use relatively large amounts of the most abundant factor resources.

Abundant factors are the relatively *cheaper* factors. In a labor-abundant and capital-scarce country, wages are relatively low and the interest rate relatively high. Goods requiring relatively large amounts of the relatively abundant factor services will therefore tend to be comparatively cheaper than other goods. Thus, a labor-abundant country, with low wage rates, can produce such articles as hand-loomed rugs more cheaply than another country which is labor-scarce and high-wage. A capital-abundant country finds its comparative advantage in capital-intensive products; a land-abundant country in land-intensive goods.

3   The Benefits of Trade

Free trading opportunities yield exchange efficiencies, realized through different marginal valuations on given goods and services. For example, let the ratio of the *marginal utilities* of two goods X and Y for two individuals A and B in pretrade isolation have the following relationship:

$$\frac{MU_X}{(MU_Y)}_A > \frac{MU_X}{(MU_Y)}_B$$

This states that individual A places a greater marginal valuation on X, compared to Y, than does individual B.

Each individual can increase his total utility through trading with the other. A trades some of his stock of good Y for good X, B some good X for good Y.

These benefits result from the exchange of *given stocks* of goods. Similar, but separate, benefits can be realized from specialization in production If each country specializes in those goods and services in which it has a comparative advantage, the total output of goods and services will be increased because resources are reallocated where they are more productive.

Other benefits of trade include the opportunity to consume goods and services that otherwise would be unavailable. Certain things produced in one country cannot be duplicated physically in another; only through international trade can the residents of all countries enjoy the products of all countries.

Free trade also keeps domestic markets competitive: in economic isolation from the rest of the world, a given industry in a country may tend strongly toward monopoly or highly restrictive oligopoly, with the adverse social effects enumerated in Chapter 16. In the presence of foreign products, however, the degree of control by domestic firms over output and price is weakened. The presumption is that this improves the efficiency of resource allocation within the country.

4   Factor Movements Compared to Trade

A labor-abundant country tends to specialize in producing labor-intensive products; a capital-abundant country in capital-intensive products, etc. The relative abundance of a factor makes its productive services relatively *low-priced:* wages tend to be low in labor-abundant countries, the interest rate low in capital-abundant countries, the rental on land low in land-abundant countries, etc.

To the extent that labor is attracted to the areas where wages are highest, labor has a motive to emigrate from labor-abundant to labor-scarce countries. For the same reasons, the owners of capital are motivated to send their capital to countries where the supply is relatively scarcer than at home.

It follows that factor movements are the consequence of the same underlying forces responsible for trade—unequal relative factor endowments. A labor-abundant country tends to export labor-intensive goods; it also tends to experience an emigration of labor. In other words, such a country either exports labor-intensive goods or labor itself. Similarly, a capital-abundant country tends either to export capital-intensive goods, or capital itself.

Trade and factor movements are substitutes for one another. Instead of the United States exporting industrial equipment to India, capital may move to India for the local production of the equipment, thereby reducing the demand for American equipment exports. On the other hand, the export of equipment to India would reduce the relative scarcity of capital in India, lessening the motivation of American capital to move there.

5 Effects of Trade and Factor Movements On Income Distribution

Both trade and factor movements reduce the relative scarcity of a country's relatively abundant factor. Indeed, this is the fundamental source of the benefits of specialization in production or the movement of factors.

Factor movements from abundant to scarce areas obviously reduce the initial imbalance. Trade, less obviously, has the same effect. The import of labor-intensive products reduces the demand in that country for labor. Although the supply of labor is not affected in an absolute sense, its economic scarcity is reduced.

As a factor becomes relatively more or less scarce, the price of its productive services becomes relatively higher or lower. Fundamentally, this is because its marginal productivity is affected positively or negatively. Correspondingly, the functional distribution of income, as described in Chapter 19, is changed. Thus, even though the real national income of a country is increased by trade or factor movements, the income yielded by the relatively scarce factor tends to decrease. At the same time, the income yielded by the relatively abundant factor tends to increase.

6 Trade and Factor Controls

Although international trade and factor movements yield great benefits, various artificial controls interfering with the freedom of trade and factor movements are present. A variety of reasons—economic, political, and social—are advanced to justify these controls. While certain arguments for tariffs, quotas, immigration restrictions, etc., have a valid economic base, others have less convincing arguments. Moreover, nearly all of the former are valid only from a national, as opposed to a cosmopolitan, point of view; others are even narrowly based on the interests of particular groups within the national economy.

D   CONFUSIONS TO AVOID

1   Absolute and Comparative Costs

International trade is based on *comparative* cost differences, not *absolute* differences. Even if one country could produce all goods and services at a lower cost, it would still be true that the costs of producing certain goods and services would be relatively higher than in other countries; this is all that is relevant as an economic basis for specialization and trade.

2   The Nation versus the World

It can be proved that international trade is beneficial, as compared to a state of national economic isolation (*autarky*). It can also be shown that, from the point of view of the world as a whole, free trade is preferable to restricted trade. However, from the national standpoint of *individual* countries, while it can be proved that some trade is better than no trade, it is not necessarily true that free trade is preferable to restricted trade. For example, under certain conditions a country may be able to act like a monopolist in its international trading relations, and obtain a larger share of the gain from trade by imposing tariffs or quotas which improve its terms of trade. However, even if the special conditions making this possible were to exist, the desire to exploit the opportunity should be tempered by the knowledge that any benefits realized would be at the expense of other countries.

3   The Individual versus the Nation

Some individuals are nearly certain to be better off without international trade, or with the protection of tariffs or quotas than with free trade. For example, the owners of the relatively scarce factor resources might enjoy higher income with no trade or restricted trade.

This raises difficult social questions about whether trade, or at least free trade, is desirable from a national (or world) point of view, since there is no objective way of comparing the gains and losses of different individuals. The resolution of this problem by modern economics is as follows: the national welfare can be said to be served by trade if those who gain from it would be able to compensate those who lose from it and still remain better off. Since trade increases the real national income in the aggregate, such compensation is possible, leaving everyone as well or better off than without trade; it is in this real sense that it can be concluded that trade promotes the nation's welfare.

CHAPTER **22** ECONOMIC GROWTH

A   PRINCIPLES

1   Meaning of Growth

Economic growth means an increase in the productive capacity of an economy. It is usually measured by the rate of increase in real national income per head of population; this determines the improvements in the standard of living.

2   Long-Run Perspective

In the short run, the real national income is dependent upon the degree of utilization of a given productive capacity, which in turn is determined by the level of aggregate demand. In the long run, the real national income is basically related to the growth in productive capacity, even though short-term cyclical fluctuations influence this growth. Hence, growth is essentially a long-run phenomenon, to be measured over several-year periods or decades.

3   Elements of Growth

Growth is the result of many different forces—social and cultural as well as economic. The economic requirements for growth include as major elements one or more of the following:

increases in the *quantity* of land or capital relative to the size of
    the population,

improvements in the economic *quality* of resources,
more *efficient* utilization of resources, and
technological advances.

4 Quantity of Land or Capital

Except by discovery or conquest, the quantity of *land* available to a country is *fixed;* its quality, however, can be transformed through productive effort.

Capital, on the other hand, is capable of quantitative change. Capital formation requires saving and investment. The ability to save is a function of real income. Low-income countries are therefore caught in a vicious circle of poverty: low income → small saving → low capital formation → low income. One possible way out of the circle is through foreign aid.

5 Qualitative Improvements

The productive quality of land can be improved through irrigation, swamp drainage, fertilization, crop rotation, etc.

The productive quality of labor can be raised by investment in educational and training facilities (investment in "human capital"), measures to eradicate diseases, improved nutrition, etc.

6 Efficiency

The *efficiency* of resource utilization may be improved through the reform of institutions, public and private, and the adoption of new cultural and social attitudes and practices.

7 Technology

Technological improvements require the acquisition of the knowledge, the means (chiefly capital and skilled labor and management) and the will to change old techniques and adopt new ones.

8 Population Growth and Economic Growth

Except for a very few underpopulated areas—and for already developed countries—a major barrier to economic growth is the tendency for standard-of-living improvements to be eroded by increases in population. This *Malthusian* tendency is especially present when there is a conjunction of high birth rates and high death rates.

B CONCEPTS

1 Measurement of Growth

The *rate of economic growth* is best measured by calculating the average annual rate of increase in real national income (that is, money national income corrected for price-level changes) divided by the rate of increase in population over a reasonably long period of time—five or ten years. Data for shorter periods of time are likely to give a distorted picture because of short-run cyclical fluctuations.

2 Cyclical Fluctuations

Cyclical fluctuations refer to the year-to-year fluctuations of economic activity through the long-run trend. These are closely related, though not identical, with the rate of growth (see Chapter 6).

3 Capital

By *capital* is meant *produced* means of production. (In a broader sense, capital is the stock of goods in existence, including consumer goods; in the present context it is useful to confine the concept to *producers'* capital.) It consists physically of tools, machinery, buildings, and all similar types of plant and equipment.

4 Saving and Investment

Saving is the act of not consuming current income. *Investment* uses the resources released by saving to add to the stock of capital.

5 Technology

Technology is the application of knowledge to production processes. Technological advances result from putting existing knowledge to practical use or through discovery and application of new knowledge.

6 Efficiency

Efficiency may be either technical or economic. *Technical efficiency* refers to the maximization of physical output from the application of given inputs, or the minimization of the physical quantity of inputs used to produce a given output. Technical efficiency is within the domain of the engineer.

Economic efficiency, as related to the production process, is achieved by choosing among the various technically possible combinations that group of inputs which *minimizes costs.* (The rule for the least-cost combination is stated in Chapter 15.) More generally, economic efficiency relates to the allocation of resources among alternative uses and is a function of the overall organization of the society.

7 Malthusian Theory of Population

Thomas Malthus, a British economist of the early 19th century, believed that food supply tends to increase at an arithmetic rate (1, 2, 3, 4,...), while population grows at a geometric rate (1, 2, 4, 8,...). In short, population tends to outgrow means of subsistence, leading to famine, disease, war, and other "natural" checks to population size. The long-run equilibrium wage, therefore, is one that barely provides subsistence for the worker.

C DISCUSSION

1 The Formation of Capital

Unless loans or grants are received from the outside world, capital cannot be formed without saving. In the absence of saving, all income, by definition, is consumed. (For present purposes, the role of government may either be ignored, or taxes included as *saving* to the extent that they finance public investment or are not spent by governments, and as *consumption* so far as they finance public consumption.) If all immediate production is currently consumed, nothing is left for adding to the stock of plant and equipment.

However, the act of saving is not in itself sufficient for the creation of capital. As described in Chapter 3, saving is a leakage in the income-expenditure stream, and unless it is matched by an equivalent amount of planned investment expenditure, it results in a decrease in the national income rather than in an increase in the productive capacity of the economy.

A perennial problem in highly developed economies is to maintain investment at a high enough level to take full advantage of the relatively large amounts of saving generated by high-income levels. The short-run aspect of this problem is that of maintaining full employment, while the long-run goal is that of maximum growth.

The problem of less-developed countries is quite different. Because of low per capita incomes, saving is small. On the other hand, the stock of capital is low in such countries, and its marginal productivity is consequently high. In any event, in the drive for economic development, the need and demand for capital is great. This is part of the "vicious circle of poverty"—the trap in which low-income countries find themselves.

One possible exit from the trap is through foreign aid. In effect, foreign aid is a process of transferring part of the saving of more highly developed countries to less-developed countries. The transfer takes the institutional form of loans and grants, but is effected in *real* terms in the form of goods and services.

2   Qualitative Improvements

In all countries, but more especially in low-income countries, the productive quality of resources can be greatly improved. Land is frequently abused through overuse, insufficient fertilization, and improper crop rotation, while large stretches may be outside productive use altogether because of arid conditions, flooding, etc. The greatest area for qualitative improvements, however, is in labor, where productivity is directly related to the level of education and training and the physical state of workers. An illiterate and poorly trained labor force, or one suffering from undernourishment or endemic disease, has a productivity far below its potential.

It should be noted that improvements in the quality of resources usually require investment, in the case of labor, in "human capital." Saving again, therefore, is an important constraint.

3   Economic Efficiency

The economic efficiency of a society is a function of many variables, sociocultural as well as economic. Economic activity takes place within a framework of established institutions and prevailing attitudes. If a price system for allocating resources is present, its potential efficiency may be undermined by monopolistic market structures, immobility of resources, an unstable monetary system, a poor tax system, etc.—frequently encountered characteristics of less-developed countries. To the extent that the government plays an important economic role, corrupt and incompetent administration is a severe constraint.

Such things as the land-tenure system also may have significant implications. In many underdeveloped countries, the greatest part of the land is owned by a few wealthy persons, with cultivation undertaken by tenant farmers under oppressive conditions. The redistribution of land ownership may in such cases be a necessary device for motivating more efficient production.

Finally, social and cultural values and attitudes can exert a crucial influence. Commitment to traditional ways of doing things, the division of society into rigid class and occupational groups, averision to hard work, etc. constitute serious barriers to economic growth.

4 Technological Improvements

Technological advances are potentially one of the most fruitful sources of economic growth. *All* resources can be made more productive if more advanced techniques and processes are employed. Consider the very rapid increase in agricultural productivity in the United States: in large part it is due to such things as hybrid seeds, stock breeding according to modern principles of eugenics, the rise of pesticides and weed-killers, and similar components of technological advances. In the industrial area, computer programming and automated factories are outstanding recent examples of technological advance.

5 Population Growth

If population increases at the same rate as total production, per capita real income remains static. In countries that are not already overpopulated, population increases may contribute to growth in per capita income by providing a larger market; this permits economices of scale through the advantages of greater division of labor and specialization. But for countries with an above-optimum population, further increases constitute a drag on economic growth.

The most serious potential of population growth as a barrier to economic growth exists in countries with high death rates and high birth rates—a typical situation in less-developed countries. This creates a threat to economic growth, for any decrease in the death rate because of improved living conditions immediately leads to an increase in population. Only if the birth rate is brought down as the death rate diminishes can the increase in population be restrained and the Malthusian obstacle to economic growth removed.

D CONFUSIONS TO AVOID

1 Cyclical Fluctuations versus Growth

Year-to-year changes in per capita real income over two- or three-year periods are likely to give a distorted view of an economy's growth. The reason is that from one year to the next, the national income may undergo fairly sharp cyclical fluctuations independent of the long-run trend (see Chapter 6). Moreover, the determinants of short-run fluctuations are quite different from the determinants of long-run growth.

2   Benefits and Costs of Growth

For most countries, economic growth is the road to the "Promised Land," the only route for raising the standard of living. It would be erroneous, however, to think that there are no costs involved.

For example, capital formation is in most cases a basic requirement for growth to be realized. But capital formation in turn requires saving, which means foregoing present consumption. In effect, saving involves a trade-off of present for future consumption. The sacrifice of present consumption is a real cost to bear, especially for countries with low per capita incomes and low standards of living.

Other costs of growth include the disruption of familiar cultural patterns—as caused by urbanization and industrialization—and the emergence of a host of new problems, such as the disappearance of traditional jobs and the appearance of technological unemployment. As nearly always when discussing economic changes, benefits have to be weighed against costs in assessing the desirability of growth.

Ability-to-pay principle of taxation, 163
Acceleration
  effect, 48
  principle, 50
Administered prices, 131–32
Aggregate demand
  and income equilibrium
    conditions, 25–39
  and inflation, 41–42, 45
  role of, 28
  and unemployment, 41
Aggregate expenditure
  components of, 17–18
  and the national income equation, 17
Autonomous expenditure, 33

Balance of payments
  accounts, 86
  deficit, 85, 91
  definition of, 84, 86, 91
  equilibrium and disequilibrium, 85,
    87, 89, 90, 91
  and the exchange rate, 85
  payments, 86
  receipts, 86
Balanced budget multiplier, 53–54,
  57–58
Bank deposits, 62, 65
  creation of, 65–66, 72–74
  different meanings of, 66
  limitations on creation of, 68
  nature of, 63
  supply of, 66
Benefit principle of taxation, 163
Bilateral monopoly, 148–49, 152
Budget
  balance and the national income, 54, 57
  deficit, 54, 59
  flexibility, 60
  surplus, 54, 59
Business cycle
  cyclical fluctuations, 47, 48–49

  implications, 52
  lower turning point, 47
  phases, 49
  upper turning point, 47

Capital
  definition of, 142, 176
  formation of, 177
    and foreign aid, 178
  supply of, 140, 147–48
    and investment, 148
    and saving, 146
Capitalization, 147
Cartels, 128
Clearing balance, 72
Comparative advantage
  and absolute advantage, 167, 172
  basis of, 165
  and disadvantage, 167
  and factor endowments, 169–70
  law of, 165, 168–69
Consumption, 17, 19–20
  function, 20–21, 23
Costs
  constant, 123
  decreasing, 123
  fixed, 110
  increasing, 123
  least, 117–18, 123, 124
  long-run, 116, 120, 124
  marginal, 109
  minimum, 124
  and productivity, 116, 120
  short run, 116, 121–22
  and supply, 122–23
  total, 110
  variable, 110
Countercyclical
  fiscal policy, 53 ff.
  monetary policy, 77, 82
Currency, 64, 65
  absence of controls on, 68, 71

appreciation, 90
circulation, 64-65
depreciation, 85, 88, 90
devaluation, 85
Cyclical fluctuations. *See* Business cycle

Deflationary gap, 41, 42-44, 45-46, 58
Demand
  aggregate, 28
  bank deposits, 61, 63, 66
  changes in, 106, 140, 144
  of consumers, 101
  curve, 94, 101, 104, 129, 132, 138
  determinants of, 105
  for factor services, 138-41,
    142-44, 150
  kinked, 128, 130
  law of supply and, 92, 96 ff., 138, 142
  for money, 76-83
  and price, 136
  price elasticity of, 94, 101
  schedule, 77, 93, 141
  shift in, 78, 105-6, 140, 144
  versus quantity demanded, 93, 100
Diminishing marginal utility, 101-2,
  103-4
Diminishing returns. *See also* Variable
  Proportions
  law of, 115
  and returns to scale, 124
Discount rate
  definition, 71
  as instrument of control, 69, 75
Disequilibrium. *See also* Equilibrium
  in the balance of payments, 85, 88, 90
  and changes in income, 31
  income, 25
Disposable personal income, 20-21
Distribution of income
  effects of trade and factor
    movements on, 171
  role of government in, 161-62

Economic growth
  benefits and costs of, 180
  elements of, 174-75
  meaning of, 174
  measurement of, 176
  and population growth, 175
Economic theory, nature of, 4
Economies of scale
  external, 119-20, 125

internal, 119-20, 122, 124-25
Efficiency
  determinants of, 178-79
  technical versus economic, 176-77
Elasticity, income
  of demand, 103
Elasticity, price, 92, 94, 101-2
  arc, 95
  coefficient of, 95
  of demand for factor services, 139,
    141, 143-46
  determinants of, 105
  expenditure test of, 96
  point, 95
  and price-quantity changes, 98-100
  and slope of demand curve, 100
  of supply, 140, 144
Employment. *See also* Unemployment
  and fiscal policy, 53 ff.
  full, 42
  and price stability, 55
Entry
  closed, 130
  free, 130, 134
  restricted, 130
Equilibrium
  balance of payments, 85, 91
  and desired income, 30
  income, 25-30
  output, 132
  partial analysis of, 147
  price, 92, 96, 132
  rate of exchange, 89
  in short and long run, 113-14
Exchange rate, foreign
  and the balance of payments, 85, 89
  depreciation, 88
  devaluation, 88
  equilibrium, 85, 89
Expenditure
  actual versus planned, 27, 53
  aggregate, 19
  autonomous, 33, 35, 39
  induced, 33, 35, 39
  test of elasticity of demand, 96
Exports, 18, 34, 165
External effects, 160, 163

Factor endowments, 167
Factor markets
  interrelationship with product
    markets, 152

Factor movements, international, 166
   compared to trade, 170–71
   controls over, 166, 171–72
   effects of on income distribution,
      165, 171
   meaning of, 167–68
   relationship to trade, 166
Federal Reserve Banks, 65, 68–70
Federal Reserve notes, 64–65
Federal Reserve System, 69–72, 74–75
Foreign aid
   and capital formation, 178
Foreign exchange. *See also* Exchange
      rate, foreign
   demand and supply of, 86–87
   and the balance of payments, 84, 88
Functional distribution of income, 153,
      155–56
Functions, 5–6

GNP. *See* Gross national product
Gold
   as dollar "backing," 67
   inflow, 88
   international monetary reserves, 89
   outflow, 88
Government expenditure
   and aggregate expenditure, 33
   principles of, 162–63
   roles of, 53–56, 158
Graphs
   construction of, 7
   illustrated, 7–10
Gross national product, 18–19

Imperfect competition, 126 ff.
   effects of on income distribution,
      154, 156
Imports, 18, 34, 165
Income. *See also* National income
   functional distribution of, 153
   personal distribution of, 154, 156
Income elasticity of demand, 103
Indivisibilities, 120
Induced expenditure, 33–34, 36, 38
Inflation
   cost-push, 41
   demand-pull, 42–46, 58–59
   and fiscal policy, 53
   meaning of, 42
Inflationary gap, 42–46,
      58–59

Interest rate
   and aggregate expenditure, 80
   and capitalized value, 147
   definition, 79
   determinants of, 76–77, 81–82
International trade
   benefits of, 166, 170, 172
   compared to factor movements,
      170–71
   effects of on income distribution, 171
   and factor controls, 171–72
Investment
   and capital, 140
   component of aggregate expenditure, 33
   expected rate of return, 80
   expenditure, 17, 23, 38, 51, 52, 80
   and government expenditure, 23
   meaning of, 24

"Kinked" demand curve, 128, 130, 135

Labor
   definition of, 142
   supply, 140, 144–45
Land
   rent, 146
   supply of, 140, 146
Leakages, 25–29, 33, 55
Long run
   costs, 122, 124
   definition of, 110
   equilibrium, 113–14
   productivity and costs, 116–17
   supply, 112–13, 117, 124

Malthus, Thomas, 177
Malthusian theory, 177
Marginal concept, 10 ff., 102
   relationship to averages, 13–14
Marginal costs, 108–9, 111–12, 120–21
Marginal efficiency of
      investment, 80
Marginal product, 118, 120–21, 141
   defined, 154
   value of, 154
Marginal productivity. *See also* Marginal
      product
   determinants of, 153, 155–56
Marginal propensity
   to consume, 34, 36, 39
   to invest, 34
   to spend, 32, 34, 36, 39

Marginal revenue, 108, 110–11,
    126–27, 129, 130–32
Marginal revenue product, 132, 141, 143
Marginal utility, 104, 107, 133
Monetary policy
    countercyclical, 77, 82
    versus fiscal policy, 77
Money
    controls over, 68 ff.
    creation of, 62, 64–66, 75
    definition of, 61
    demand for, 76, 77–78, 83
    functions of, 61–63
    and the interest rate, 81–82
    and the national income, 76,
        79–81, 83
    nature of, 61, 64, 68
    sources of, 62
    supply of, 62, 77–78
    velocity of circulation, 79
Monopolistic competition, 126
    benefits of, 128, 135
    definition, 127
    objections to, 127 ff.
    output, 127–28, 134–35
    price, 134–35
Monopoly
    benefits, 133
    bilateral, 148–49, 152
    definition, 126–27
    in factor markets, 148 ff.
    objections to, 133
    output, 126–27, 132–33, 135
    price, 132–33, 135, 137, 148
Multiplier
    and the accelerator, 52
    definition, 32
    effects, 38–39
    formula, 32, 35, 38
    magnitude of, 34–38
Monopsony, 148
    in factor markets, 149, 151
    supply of factor services
        under, 151

National debt
    and fiscal policy, 54, 59
National income. *See also* Income
    definition, 16
    equation, 17, 22–23
    equilibrium, 25–27, 29–30
    at factor costs, 16, 18

and government expenditure, 158
    measures of, 16, 18–19
    multiplier, 32, 34–38
    real and money, 16–17, 19, 23
    and taxes, 158
Net national product, 16, 18–19

Official settlements account, 86
Oligopoly
    benefits of, 129, 136
    definition, 128, 135
    demand curve, 128
    heterogeneous, 128, 136
    homogeneous, 128
    objections to, 129, 136
    output, 127–29, 135
    price, 127–29, 135, 137
    product competition, 128, 136
Open-market operations, 69, 71, 74–75
Optimum output and price, 130

Personal distribution of income, 154
    role of government in, 159
Personal income, 20
Personal income, disposable, 20
Planned obsolescence, 136
Population
    and economic growth, 175, 179
    Malthusian theory of, 177
Production function, 115, 118
Profits
    and supply, 108
    definition, 136
    economic versus business, 113
    rule for maximizing, 108, 111
Progressive taxes, 159, 161
Propensity to consume, 39
Propensity to spend, 32, 34
Proportional taxes, 159, 161
Public goods, 160, 162, 164
Pure competition, 136–37

Quotas, 168

Recession, 47, 49, 51
Regressive taxes, 159, 161
Rent, economic, 140 ff., 144, 146
Reserves, bank
    control over, 74–75
    excess, 68, 70, 73, 75
    legal, 70, 75
    and money creation, 72–75

nature of, 68–70
need for, 71–72
required, 68, 70
sources of, 68–69, 74
Returns to scale, 116, 120, 122–24

Saving
and capital formation, 140, 176–77
deposits, 63
function, 21
planned, 25–26, 28
Short run
costs, 121–22
definition of, 110
equilibrium, 113–14
supply, 111–12, 116
Stabilizers, built-in, 54–56
Structural unemployment, 41, 44
Substitution effect, 101–5
Supply
of capital, 145–46
and costs, 122–24
elasticity, 92, 94–96, 98–100
of factor services, 140, 149, 151
of labor, 144–45
of land, 146
in long run competition, 109,
112–13, 116–17
and productivity, 115
and profits, 108
and quantity supplied, 93, 100
schedule, 96
in short run competition, 108,
111–12, 116
under imperfect competition, 126 ff.

T-account, 63
Tariffs, 168
Taxation. *See also* Taxes
marginal rate of, 37
principles of, 159, 163
Taxes
functions of, 163–64
incidence and shifting of, 160,
161–62
and the multiplier, 37–38, 40
and the national income, 25 ff.
principles of, 160, 163
roles of, 158
types of, 159
Technology, 155
improvements in, 179
meaning of, 176
Terms of trade, 168
Transfer payments, 56

Unemployment
causes of, 42–45
definition of, 42, 55
and fiscal policy, 53, 58
structural, 41, 44
U.S. Bureau of Labor Statistics, 42
Utility
definition, 102
diminishing marginal, law of, 101–2
marginal, 102, 106
maximization of, 104, 107

Variable proportions. *See also*
Diminishing returns
law of, 115, 119–20

4098